Prayer in the New Testament

Books by Fred L. Fisher
Published by The Westminster Press ®

PRAYER IN THE NEW TESTAMENT
THE PURPOSE OF GOD
AND THE CHRISTIAN LIFE

PRAYER

IN THE

NEW TESTAMENT

by

Fred L. Fisher

THE WESTMINSTER PRESS
Philadelphia

PRINTED IN THE UNITED STATES OF AMERICA
PUBLISHED BY THE WESTMINSTER PRESS ®
PHILADELPHIA, PENNSYLVANIA 19107

Contents

          Bodily Posture in Prayer   177
          Wording of Prayers   179
          Place of Prayer   180
          Clothes and Prayer   181
          Fasting and Prayer   183

      Addenda: Materials for Study   186

      Notes   189

Introduction

All men pray. Not all men pray aright. These two statements justify any effort that man may make to understand the nature and way of prayer. This book is such an attempt. It is written with the firm belief that any relationship that we have with God must be regulated by the teachings of the New Testament.

What we want in our study of prayer is not the expert opinion of modern man, but the assurance or reassurance of the Word of God. Since all men of all religious opinions pray and have experiences of "answered" prayer, the material for study from that viewpoint is almost endless. Yet, for the man who wishes assurance that his prayer is pleasing to God, the material is almost without value. The relation between the prayers of men and the effects that are seemingly wrought by the prayers is so uncertain, so impossible to observe with accuracy, that such evidence is of little value. A man may pray for a storm to stop; it may stop, but did it stop *because* that man prayed as he did? The man of faith may say that it did. The skeptic may have his doubts. No one can know for certain, unless he has access to the mind of God.

If we cannot decide, on the basis of human testimony, whether a particular prayer brought particular results, how much more impossible is it, on the same basis, to chart a pathway of prayer for our lives! The man who wants to pray wants to know how to pray with the assurance that his prayer is pleasing to God, that his requests are the proper requests to make, that his spirit is the kind of spirit that will ensure prayer results. We cannot learn this from men. We must learn it from God.

7

One way we learn from God is by studying the teachings of the New Testament. This is true with respect to all matters of the Christian faith; it is especially true of the subject of prayer. It seems to me that the only way to attain assurance in prayer is to search out the teachings of the New Testament and make them normative for our prayer life.

With this principle in mind, I have sought to study the examples of prayer in the New Testament and to derive from them the principles of Christian prayer. The result of my study has been to confirm much of that which I have always believed, that which forms the centrality of thought about prayer in the whole Christian community. But some of that which is commonly accepted has also been brought under suspicion. I have attempted to avoid dogmatism, to remain true to the teachings of the New Testament, and to leave room for difference of opinion.

I have recognized that it is impossible to lay down hard-and-fast rules about prayer. God is so gracious that he often answers in power when we pray in ways that are not wholly Christian. Rather, I have attempted to find the ideals of prayer and the most Christian ways of praying, and present them as a challenge to the man of prayer to correct and deepen his experience of communion with God.

I acknowledge my debt to those who have written and spoken of prayer. Wherever possible, I have given credit by means of footnotes to those from whom I have derived my thought. However, I am conscious that someone has probably said in one connection or another everything that I have to say. Whatever plagiarism may exist in the book is unconscious on my part, but I am aware that many of the thoughts, which I think are mine, are the subconscious treasure of years of study and listening.

As an addenda I have listed the materials for study that may be found in the New Testament—all of them as far as I was able. It could be that this will be the most valuable part of the book, that the reader will prefer to do his own study and reach his own conclusions rather than follow the intricacies of the author's thought.

If this is true, I will be all the happier for it. The best book ever written on prayer is the New Testament. The best way to understand prayer is through a study of the New Testament.

FRED L. FISHER

Golden Gate Baptist Theological Seminary
Mill Valley, California

Theology of Prayer—Synopsis

Our conception of God controls the contents, the method, and the conditions of prayer.

The necessary theological presuppositions of prayer are that God is personal, immanent, powerful, and susceptible to human influence through prayer. Each of these necessary presuppositions of prayer is a basic teaching of the New Testament.

Prayer likewise assumes that man is weak and dependent on some power outside himself for the fulfillment of his life. This also is a basic teaching of the New Testament.

New Testament teachings, in laying the foundation for prayer, go beyond the necessary assumptions of prayer. The Fatherhood of God and his delight in giving good gifts encourage us to pray. Further, the teaching that God is the source and giver of all that man receives stresses the duty and privilege of prayer.

I

The Theology of Prayer

Prayer begins with God; what God is and does is the controlling factor in prayer. This must be, since prayer is the approach of man to God as he seeks God's fellowship, favor, help, and approval. Intercourse with God can never spring from what man is, desires, hopes, or purposes. A study of prayer in the New Testament must therefore begin with a study of the theology of prayer, the fundamental conceptions of God that form the foundation for prayer and that determine the vital elements of prayer. The way a man prays reveals what he believes about God[1]; what he believes about God determines how he prays.

First, what God is dictates the content of prayer, the things that we may properly ask God to do. The range of requests that may be addressed to any person is determined by that person's character and power. We do not ask a minister to share in a poker game, nor a beggar to lend us a thousand dollars. In the same way, the character and nature of God must determine what we may ask God to give or do. Chiang Kai-shek, it is said, once asked his mother-in-law to pray for the destruction of the Japanese nation. She replied that such a prayer would be unworthy of Chiang and that it would be an insult to God.

The character of God dictates the content of our requests; it dictates the method of prayer as well. A Biblical example of this fundamental truth is found in the taunts of Elijah as the prophets of Baal tried to call fire down from heaven to consume their sacrifice. "And at noon Elijah mocked them, saying, 'Cry aloud, for he is a god; either he is musing, or he has gone aside, or he is

on a journey, or perhaps he is asleep and must be awakened.' "
(I Kings 18:27.) The prophets of Baal accepted this ironic description of their god; "they cried aloud, and cut themselves after
their custom with swords and lances, until the blood gushed out
upon them" (v. 28). In contrast to the frenzied efforts by the
prophets of the false god, Elijah quietly prayed: "O Lord, God
of Abraham, Isaac, and Israel, let it be known this day that thou
art God in Israel, and that I am thy servant, and that I have done
all these things at thy word. Answer me, O Lord, answer me, that
this people may know that thou, O Lord, art God, and that thou
hast turned their hearts back" (vs. 36–37). What a contrast in the
conception of God! What a contrast in methods of prayer! One is
the frenzied effort to awaken a sleeping god; the other is the
quiet request of one who knows his God and does God's will.
The contrast in the prayers arose out of the contrasting conceptions of the nature of the deity to whom the prayer was addressed.

The character of God must always be the determining factor in
the method of prayer. Jesus made the nature of God the basis for
his warning against the hypocrisy of the Pharisees (Matt. 6:5–6)
and the empty babbling of the Gentiles (vs. 7–8). Since God sees
in secret and knows the needs of the heart before the request is
made, Jesus said, there is no need for ostentatious display or for
empty repetitions.

Finally, the nature of God determines the conditions under
which our petitions to him may be granted. In the New Testament, for instance, no trace is found of any attempt to present a
bribe to God in order to win his compliance with our request.
This is in startling contrast to the practice of pagan religions and
even to the record of prayers in the Old Testament. It is reported
that Jacob promised, "The Lord shall be my God," and "Of all
that thou givest me I will give the tenth to thee," as inducements
to gain the protection and providence of God in his journey (Gen.
28:20–22). These vows sound very much like an attempt to bar-
gain with God, an attitude that is far removed from the communion of Jesus with his Father and the teachings of the New
Testament on prayer. The basic truth is that the changed concep-

tion of prayer which we find in the New Testament is based on a changed conception of God.

What are the focal points in our conception of God in relation to our practice of prayer? What must man believe about God before he can or will pray? What are the *necessary* presuppositions of the practice of prayer? If one were to ask this question philosophically, it is very likely that he would conclude that before prayer can be a real factor in a man's life, he must believe that God is personal, immanent, powerful, and susceptible to the influence of men in some sense. Of course, prayer would also assume something about man in his existence; it would assume that man is weak and finite and must rely on some force or power outside himself for his personal fulfillment and the achievement of his highest aims. Thus, we see, there are five factors in the theology of prayer—four theological assumptions and one anthropological. Let us examine these factors to see why they are necessary presuppositions to the practice of prayer and then subject each one to the searchlight of New Testament teachings to see if the New Testament gives an adequate theological basis for prayer.

First, it would seem self-evident that the personality of God is a necessary presupposition of prayer. At least in the sense of petition, prayer rests upon the belief that the God to whom we pray is personal. It is true that some practices of men which are called prayer are purely subjective. It cannot be denied that there is the possibility of some degree of inspiration and help through introspection, through the contemplation of the beauties and grandeur of nature, through the finer works of men, or through a consideration of the movements of history. Such inspiration, however, can hardly merit the name of prayer. Though the New Testament itself records the futile petition of men to the mountains and rocks to fall on them and hide them from the wrath of God (Rev. 6:16), in his sane moments no man thinks of praying to the objects of nature, less so to himself, and certainly not to the figures of history. Men seek to exercise self-discipline to make full use of the resources that are inherent within them. They seek to control and manipulate nature, to gain from it the help that nature may give. They seek to emulate the qualities of great men of the past in order to achieve as they achieved. When we pray, however, we pray to one who meets us on personal terms, one who can respond by an act of the will to our plea. We may pray about ourselves or about the forces of nature, but we pray to God, and the God to whom we pray must be personal.

Does the New Testament justify the Christian claim that God is personal? To ask the question is to answer it. Woven into the warp and woof of the New Testament is the belief that God is personal, that man can and does have personal relations with God. Of course, we recognize that the language of the Bible is an attempt to express the inexpressible, an attempt to understand the God who reveals himself to us. The language of the Bible, even the application of the term "personal" to God, is necessarily inadequate. Every term that we use is figurative, or as Emil Brunner says, "parabolic."[2] God makes himself visible to men in personal terms, and it is always personal terms, such as "Father," "Lord," "King," and "Judge," that are "drawn from the finite sphere to express the infinite."[3] Never, neither in the Old Testament nor in the New, do we find the application of abstractions or of names of objects to God. This all points to the essentially personal nature of the God of Christianity.

The primary evidence of God's personal nature is found, however, in the fact that the supreme self-disclosure of God took place in a man, the man Christ Jesus. In answer to the request of Philip, "Lord, show us the Father, and we shall be satisfied," Jesus answered: "Have I been with you so long, and yet you do not know me, Philip? He who has seen me has seen the Father" (John 14:8-9). The relation of Jesus and the apostles to God was not the relation of "I-it" but the relation of "I-Thou." "God comes to us in person in Jesus Christ, and only in this event is He our real Thou."[4] Even the famous trilogy of Johannine ideas, which have often been taken to be abstract utterances about the nature of God, turn out on closer examination to present God in personal terms. These are: "God is spirit" (John 4:24); "God is light" (I John 1:5); and "God is love" (I John 4:8). We notice that in each instance the statement about the nature of God is given to enforce a personal demand on the life of the man who seeks to worship and have fellowship with him. Since God is spirit, true worship must be in "spirit and truth," that is, personal. Since God is light, fellowship with God demands righteousness— a moral, personal quality—from man. Since God is love, we must love our brethren. In each case, the terms are seen to refer to the personal characteristics of God rather than being an attempt to define God in abstract terms. The first necessary presupposition of the practice of prayer is thus seen to be a fundamental teaching of the New Testament.

Again, a life of prayer demands a conception of the immanence of God, the fact that God moves and acts on the plane of human affairs. The God of the deist, who sits in lonely isolation, transcending the universe and watching it run its course, may inspire awe and fear. He could never inspire prayer. The Jews had such a conception of God, especially the Sadducees. Perhaps this explains why prayer never became the personal, dynamic force in Jewish life which it attained in the Christian communities. Certainly it is true that the closer God is to us, the more real he is in our consciousness, the more we are inclined to pray. Perhaps the most impressive reality in the life of Jesus was his constant awareness of the presence of the living God. This awareness, more than anything else, accounts for the fact that he was preeminently a man of prayer.

Does the New Testament justify the belief that God is immanent—that he does work in human life? Is it true that though this world is not yet his Kingdom, it is his workshop? This truth is so axiomatic in the New Testament that it hardly needs to be argued. Jesus told the Jews, "My Father is working still, and I am working" (John 5:17). Paul believed that it was the effective presence of God which gave the results in his own preaching ministry (I Cor. 3:7). He told the Athenians, "He is not far from each one of us" (Acts 17:27), and urged Christians to yield the members of their body to God for the work of righteousness (Rom. 6:19). He asserted that "in everything God works for good

with those who love him, who are called according to his purpose" (Rom. 8:28). God is never thought of as an absentee God
nor as a stranger or an alien in the world. Though Christian
thought never wavered at the point of the transcendence of God,
neither did it doubt his constant, living, dynamic presence in the
world.

The third theological presupposition to prayer is belief that
God has the power to make a difference in the life of the individual worshiper as well as in the course of human history. Before
we can ask God to act in our behalf, we must believe that he can
do so. One does not ask a pauper for money, because he knows
that the pauper has none. One does not ask a child for business
advice, because he knows that this is beyond the power of the
child to give. In all our requests to men, we seek out the persons
who are able to grant what we ask before we ask it. The same
principle must hold true in our life of prayer. We will not ask
God to do what we consider to be beyond his power to achieve.
Thus, to pray we must believe in the power of God to make a
difference in our lives.

Does the New Testament justify such a belief? The answer
is not difficult to find; a conviction of the power of God to change
lives and influence the course of world history is found on nearly
every page of the New Testament. "Jesus looked at them and
said, 'With men it is impossible, but not with God; for all things
are possible with God.'" (Mark 10:27.) Paul did not hesitate to
put his case and the case of his fellow shipmates in the hands
of God. When God assured him that he would preserve them
from destruction, Paul said with the confident faith that is
characteristic of New Testament men, "I have faith in God"
(Acts 27:25).

The Ephesian letter, in an exalted benediction, says, "Now to
him who by the power at work within us is able to do far more
abundantly than all that we ask or think, to him be glory in the
church and in Christ Jesus to all generations, for ever and ever.
Amen" (Eph. 3:20–21). According to the faith of New Testament men, it is God who sustains the universe, sends the rain
and the sunshine, protects the fowls of the air, saves sinners,

sustains saints, gives power for service, comforts the bereaved, determines the rulers of the nations of the world, raises the dead, and overcomes the powers of evil. There is nothing that is thought to be beyond his power. Certainly there is nothing that man can think to ask that is beyond the power of God to give.

In the fourth place, the man of prayer must believe that God is somehow susceptible to influence by the prayer of men. It is against the nature of man to persist in any practice for long unless he believes that it will in some way make a difference. One might, in the extremities of life, be impelled to cry out to God without a real confidence in the efficacy of prayer, hoping that prayer may help but not really believing that it will. However, such an attitude toward God and the efficacy of prayer is very unlikely to be the foundation of a life of prayer. If the purpose of God is conceived of as something that is fixed and unchangeable, something that will come to pass regardless of what men may do, if man's faith in God is fatalistic, man will not be inspired to pray. If the unchangeableness of God is thought of in terms of his immobility, man will not be inspired to pray. One of the pressing problems of man's religious life is to find a way to maintain his faith in a purposeful God and at the same time to feel that his praying will make a difference of some kind either in the purpose, desire, or action of God. There are groups of Christians who refuse to pray for the salvation of the lost because they feel that prayer in this respect would be in vain. Others, perhaps not because of a formal doctrine but because of a personal feeling, refuse to pray for anything at all for the same reason. It is true, then, to say that man must believe in the susceptibility of God to human influence if prayer is to become a meaningful experience in his life.

Does the New Testament justify our thinking that God acts in response to human prayer in ways in which he would not or could not otherwise act? The answer to this question is in the affirmative. Jesus and his disciples believed that God did answer prayer; they believed that "prayer changes things." Jesus admonished his disciples, "Ask, and it will be given you" (Matt. 7:7); and he promised, "Every one who asks receives" (v. 8). The

implication of this teaching is that there is a cause-effect relationship between asking of God and receiving from God. Failure to
ask will result in failure to receive; asking will result in receiving.
It seems impossible to understand this teaching of the Master in
any other way than to suppose that he believed that our prayers
do make a difference in God's action, that the Father is susceptible
to human influence. James makes the negative side of this
teaching explicit in his statement: "You do not have, because you
do not ask" (James 4:2).

In the continuing history of the early Christian movement, the
records are so written as to present belief in a cause-effect relation
between prayer and God's action. The first church was commanded to tarry in Jerusalem until "clothed with power from on
high" (Luke 24:49). The action of the people of Jerusalem in
response to this command showed that they interpreted this as
a command not only to stay in Jerusalem but to pray, for "all
these with one accord devoted themselves to prayer" (Acts 1:14).
The recorded result of this prayer meeting was that on the Day of
Pentecost, attended by wondrous signs, "they were all filled with
the Holy Spirit and began to speak in other tongues, as the
Spirit gave them utterance" (Acts 2:4). This record of the initial
endowment of the church is so written as to leave unavoidable
the conclusion that the coming of the Spirit was in response to
the prayer of the church.

Two other incidents in the early history of Christians may
suffice to illustrate this underlying assumption of the entire
New Testament. One is the preaching of the gospel to Cornelius
by Peter (Acts, ch. 10.) The initial movement in the story is
the appearance of the angel to instruct Cornelius to send for
Peter so that the gospel might be proclaimed to him. Cornelius is
described as a man who "prayed constantly to God" (v. 2), and
the angel told him, "Your prayers and your alms have ascended as
a memorial before God" (v. 4). As the messengers made their way
to Joppa, "Peter went up on the housetop to pray" (v. 9). During
the session of prayer, a vision came to Peter that was designed to
offset the racial prejudice that still existed in his heart and cause

him to respond to the appeal of the messengers. When Peter arrived and Cornelius recounted his experience, Peter exclaimed, "Truly I perceive that God shows no partiality" (v. 34). In this story, prayer is shown to play a vital part in the action of God in bringing the preacher and the hearer together, so that salvation could be wrought in the heart and home of Cornelius and that the missionary spirit could be created in the heart of the apostle. The release of Peter from prison is a story of like meaning. The keynote of the story is found in the record: "So Peter was kept in prison; but earnest prayer for him was made to God by the church" (Acts 12:5). As a result, Peter was released by an angel of the Lord and restored to the church.

The New Testament teaches that God does answer the prayers of men, that he acts in response to prayer in ways in which he could not or would not otherwise have acted. However, the exact way in which prayer affects God is not discussed; it remains a problem for modern minds. To arrive at some solution to the problem, we will have to distinguish between the purpose, the desire, and the action of God. It is hardly to be thought that prayer could change the purpose of God. If it is true that God has a pretemporal, eternal purpose for human history and for the saved which is based on his own nature, grace, and choice, it is difficult to see how prayer would be able to change that purpose. That God has such a purpose lies at the heart of the New Testament. "The very idea of God, at least the Christian idea, depends upon belief that God is working out his own purpose in the world. . . . In his relationship with the world, God cannot be thought of as one who follows along and accomplishes all the good he can as conditions permit. He, if he is absolute and ultimate, must be the creative factor in world history. He must be working out a purpose; he must have a goal. It is impossible to retain any real faith in God and believe that anything can ultimately thwart the accomplishment of his purpose."[5] We would have to say, then, that human prayer cannot change the purpose of God.

Can prayer change the desire of God? Again, there is no

evidence in the New Testament to justify such a belief. The New Testament teaches that God is perfectly good, that he desires to give good gifts to all men. To think of changing God's desire would involve us in a contradiction of thought. Either we would have to suppose that we could persuade God to do something that is not good or suppose that he must be persuaded to do something that is good. In either case we would have to surrender our belief in the perfect goodness of God. There are some who, with a sort of childish superstition, warn us that if we pray for a thing that is not good for us, God may give it to us to our ultimate harm. Such a thought would seem utterly inconsistent with the thought of Jesus and his disciples. No, we must not hope to change the desire of God by prayer; indeed, we should not even want to do this.

Can the action of God be changed or influenced by human prayer? The answer to this must be yes. All the admonitions of the New Testament that encourage men to make definite petitions to God or to intercede with God in behalf of other men imply that God's actions are affected by prayer. If it were asked how this could be so, the answer might lie in a very human illustration. Every teacher comes to the classroom with the desire to impart knowledge and inspire growth on the part of his students. He would feel insulted if a student with a note of despair in his voice should cry out, "O teacher, please teach us." Yet, every teacher knows that teaching is impossible until some such desire, expressed or not, is aroused in the mind of the student. So long as the student does not realize his need for knowledge, he cannot be taught. Even if he realizes his need, but rebels against the effort required to learn, he cannot be taught. However, when the student desires knowledge, the way is opened for the teacher to accomplish his desire, to do what he has wanted to do all along. This is why it can be said that "prayer is to open the door and give Jesus access to our need."[6] God must await our prayer, our conscious expression of need and desire, before he can give us his best gifts. As we have seen above, the prayers of Cornelius opened the way for God to send him a messenger of salvation, an action that we must believe was always God's desire but that awaited the prayer of the sinner before it could be fulfilled. In like manner, the prayer of the elders at Antioch opened the way for God to send out his first missionaries to the Gentile world (Acts 13:2). This subject will arise again in the chapter on "petition," but the principle presented here will also control our discussion there.

Finally, a life of prayer rests upon man's conception of himself as weak and needing the help of some outside power to achieve the fulfillment of his life. This belief is more anthropological than theological in the strict meaning of the terms, but broadly speaking, it may be placed in a discussion of the theology of prayer. It should go without saying that the man who feels himself self-sufficient would never pray for help from God. He might seek the approval of God as the Pharisee did who, according to the parable of Jesus, prayed: "God, I thank thee that I am not like other men" (Luke 18:11). This parable was given to condemn those who "trusted in themselves that they were righteous and despised others" (v. 9). The example shows how impossible it is for one who truly trusts in himself to pray in the Christian sense. Of course, there is a basic contradiction between the spirit of the Pharisee and the words, "God, I thank thee." Man's sense of dependence on some power outside himself has long been recognized as an essential element of all religious practice. Certainly it is a necessary prerequisite to the practice of prayer.

Does the New Testament justify the belief that man must turn to God for the good things of life and for his own personal fulfillment? The answer to this question must be yes; man's weakness and evil is proverbial. Jesus accepted it as axiomatic that even the parents who gave good gifts to their children were fundamentally evil (Luke 11:13). Paul taught that the natural man is "by nature" a child of wrath, enslaved by sin (Eph. 2:1–3). In a poignant passage, probably autobiographical in part, Paul describes the futile attempt of the natural man to overcome his sin and achieve righteousness, an attempt that inevitably for the sensitive man leads to the cry of despair: "Wretched man that I am! Who will deliver me from this body of death?" (Rom. 7:24).

Even the Christian finds that he is not self-sufficient. Though the root-sin of rebellion against God has been overcome in his surrender to the Lordship of Christ, the battle between the Spirit and the flesh (man's lower self) continues (Gal. 5:17). All the true virtues of the Christian life are described as the "fruit of the Spirit" (v. 22), whereas the only works of the flesh, the works of man himself, are described as evil (vs. 19–21). Jesus warned his disciples that they could do nothing apart from a continuing fellowship with him (John 15:5). In the Gethsemane experience, he admonished them, "Watch and pray that you may not enter into temptation; the spirit indeed is willing, but the flesh is weak" (Mark 14:38). Interesting indeed is the close connection that exists in the New Testament between the thought of man's weakness and the admonitions to pray. Furthermore, the promises of power in service in the New Testament are always related to the promise of answered prayer (John 14:12–14), the indwelling Spirit of God (Acts 1:8), and the effective working of God through the efforts of men (I Cor. 3:5–9).

There is no foundation in the New Testament for a belief in the self-sufficiency of man. Left to himself, man is a helpless creature, enslaved by the powers of evil. He must have outside help, help from God. The answer to his need must come through the practice of prayer if it comes at all.

Given these theological foundations of prayer, man would certainly be encouraged to make prayer a constant practice of his life. If nothing more could be said than has been said about the possibilities of prayer fellowship with God, prayer would be indicated for all men. But much more can be said on the basis of New Testament teachings, most of which will be discussed in later chapters, but some of which needs to be summarized here because it properly belongs in a discussion of the theology of prayer.

One New Testament conception of God that goes beyond the necessary presuppositions of prayer is the teaching that God is the Father of the believer. This is a conception that received new meaning through the consciousness and teaching of Jesus. God was Jesus' father in a personal and individual sense, but God is also the father, in a derived sense, of all believers. Jesus sent word to the disciples, saying, "I am ascending to my Father and your Father" (John 20:17), and taught all believers to pray, "Our Father who art in heaven" (Matt. 6:9). He taught that the Father was so intimately concerned about the needs of his children that we need not inform God of our needs, "for your Father knows what you need before you ask him" (v. 8). Believers are told not to worry about the threats of men, for the God who is concerned about the sparrows values them far more highly than the birds of the air (Luke 12:6–7). He even asserts that it will no longer be necessary for him to intercede on behalf of the believer because "the Father himself loves you" (John 16:27). The thought of the Fatherhood of God is a constant emphasis of the New Testament. Of course, it describes a relationship that, for men, must always be derived. God is first of all the "God and Father of our Lord Jesus Christ," and then the "Father of mercies and God of all comfort" to those who love and honor Christ (II Cor. 1:3–4). But it is nevertheless a real relation created by our conversion and made a factor in our consciousness by the indwelling Spirit of God who, when we cry out, "Abba! Father! . . . is . . . himself bearing witness with our spirit that we are children of God" (Rom. 8:15–16). Peter assumes that it is axiomatic that the Christian invokes "as Father him who judges each one impartially" (I Peter 1:17), and therefore he admonishes his readers, "Cast all your anxieties on him, for he cares about you" (I Peter 5:7). The fact that we may approach the throne of God, as children who belong to the family of God, not merely as subjects to the Creator of the universe, is in itself an encouragement to pray.

Another basic thought about God in the New Testament that goes beyond the philosophical presuppositions of prayer is the teaching that God delights to give good gifts to men. He is not pictured as a reluctant hoarder of his blessings, but as an eager sharer of them. James describes God as one "who gives to all men generously and without reproaching" and makes this fact an encouragement to pray (James 1:5). Paul insists that God is not partial but "bestows his riches upon all who call upon him" (Rom. 10:12). Jesus argued a fortiori for the willingness of God to give, saying, "If you then, who are evil, know how to give good gifts to your children, how much more will your Father who is in heaven give good things to those who ask him!" (Matt. 7:11). He also asserted that "it is your Father's good pleasure to give you the kingdom" (Luke 12:32). The thought of God's delight in giving is sometimes challenged by a misunderstanding of two of the parables of Jesus: the parable of the reluctant friend (Luke 11:5–8) and the parable of the unjust judge (Luke 18:1–8). In both cases, however, it is to be noted that Jesus told these parables to encourage prayer. Each of them contains a contrast between the reluctance of men to give what they should give when it may be inconvenient and the willingness of the Father to give what he can give even at great cost. We are justified in saying that the New Testament teaches that God is anxious and eager to give his gifts to men.

Finally, it may be emphasized that the New Testament teaches that God is the source and giver of all spiritual blessings that man receives. Not only does he want to give, he does give. All the prayers of thanksgiving in the New Testament imply that this is true. There is no need at this point to enumerate all the things that are said to come from God. Some of them are salvation (Eph. 2:8–10), patience (Rom. 15:5–6), consolation (vs. 5–6), and hope (v. 13). In line with this thought, God is called the God of peace, i.e., the God who gives peace (Rom. 16:20; 15:33), the God of comfort (II Cor. 1:3–4), and he is designated as Savior (I Tim. 4:10) and deliverer (II Tim. 4:17–18).

We see, then, that prayer is both a need and a possibility for men. It opens the way for weak and sinful men to tap the great resources of the living God for their own blessing and benefit. It is the practice that links heaven and earth together as the sphere of man's life and saves man from the despair that would

come if he were left to himself. However, prayer is not an easy
road to a comfortable life. We do not mean to imply that the
New Testament teaches that man may cast all his burdens and
difficulties on the shoulders of God and go away without further
thought or effort, expecting to receive ready-made solutions of
life's problems. Much more is involved than this. What is involved
will become clearer, we hope, as we proceed. What has been
said justifies our proceeding, for without this foundation for
prayer, which rests primarily in the person of God, all discussion
of prayer would be meaningless.

Jesus and Prayer—Synopsis

The Gospel records of Jesus' life stress the fact that he was a man of prayer.

The Christian doctrine of the incarnation justifies us in taking the prayer life of Jesus as our example. A study of his prayers should help us to understand the nature and meaning of prayer.

His prayer of thanksgiving was a calm acknowledgment of the propriety of God's action and will.

His prayer at the grave of Lazarus sought God's glorification.

His dialogue with the Father when the Greeks sought him showed a spirit of submission. So also did his prayer in Gethsemane.

The high-priestly prayer revealed the heart of Jesus and constitutes an important guide for Christian prayer.

The prayer that his crucifiers be forgiven conformed to his teaching that we should pray for our enemies.

The prayer of dereliction showed the human agony of Jesus on the cross.

His prayer of commitment reveals how men ought to pray in the extremity of pain and death.

A study of the prayer life of Jesus illustrates the following principles of Christian prayer: habitual prayer, dependence on God, self-committal to the Father, and unwavering confidence in God's love, power, and wisdom.

II

Jesus and Prayer

A study of Christian prayer must begin with Jesus. In this respect, as in all other matters vital to Christian life, he is the supreme example. There can be no doubt that Jesus was known and remembered as a man of prayer. Hardly any other single factor in his life receives so much attention in our Gospel records as does his prayer life. There are twenty-one recorded instances of his prayer life in the four Gospels and twenty-one passages that report his teachings on the subject of prayer. This is to be compared with the forty-five times that Jesus is said to have taught and the sixteen times that he is said to have preached.[7]

Note is taken of the fact that he prayed at his baptism (Luke 3:21), at the feeding of both the five thousand (Mark 6:41; Matt. 14:19; Luke 9:16; John 6:11) and the four thousand (Mark 8:6–7), before challenging the faith of the disciples at Caesarea Philippi (Luke 9:18), at the transfiguration experience (Luke 9:28–29), before giving the model prayer (Luke 11:1), when he blessed the little children (Mark 10:13–16; Matt. 19:13), at the institution of the Lord's Supper (Mark 14:22–23; Matt. 26:26–27; Luke 22:17–19), and at the breaking of bread with the two disciples on the way to Emmaus (Luke 24:30–31).

In three passages, note is taken of Jesus' habit of prayer. Mark records that after healing Peter's mother-in-law and the multitudes on the Sabbath, "in the morning, a great while before day, he rose and went out to a lonely place, and there he prayed" (Mark 1:35). Luke records the fact that during the active part of his Galilean ministry, Jesus "continued his practice of retiring to lonely places and praying" (Luke 5:16, my translation). It is Luke also who records that before he chose the Twelve he spent the night in prayer (Luke 6:12–13). In only one place is it recorded that Jesus himself made mention of his prayer life. When he prophesied Peter's denial, he told Peter that he had prayed for him (Luke 22:31–32).

The Gospel writers give eight of the prayers of Jesus, at least in part. These are in addition to the passages cited above. His prayer of thanksgiving at the time he sent out his disciples two by two is given (Matt. 11:25–26; Luke 10:21). His prayer at the grave of Lazarus is recorded (John 11:41–42). His dialogue with God on the occasion of the coming of the Greeks to seek him is reported (John 12:27–30). Two versions of his prayer in Gethsemane are given: one is usually designated as his high-priestly prayer (John 17:1–26), the other his prayer of surrender to the will of God (Mark 14:32–42; Matt. 26:36–46; Luke 22:39–46). Finally, three prayers from the cross are recorded: the so-called prayer of dereliction (Mark 15:34; Matt. 27:46), his prayer for the forgiveness of his tormentors (Luke 23:34), and his prayer of quiet commitment of his soul to the Father (v. 46).

Jesus' teachings probably reflect his own practice of prayer. Since most of these passages will be considered in other contexts, it is not necessary at this point to discuss them. It is worthy of notice that Jesus would not have taught his disciples to practice prayer in any way in which he did not himself practice it. The lone exception, if the Christian belief in the sinlessness of Jesus is true, would be the petition in the model prayer in which the disciples were urged to ask for the forgiveness of their sins.

There can be no doubt that his disciples and the people of Judea regarded him as a man of prayer. It was his practice of prayer that led the disciples to request him to teach them to pray (Luke 11:1). It was his reputation as a man of God that led the mothers of Israel to bring their little children to him for his blessing (Mark 10:13–16; Matt. 19:13). It was his practice of prayer that inspired the assertion of Martha in the depths of her grief: "Lord, if you had been here, my brother would not have died. And even now I know that whatever you ask from God, God will give you" (John 11:21–22). Such expressions of confidence in the prayer life and power of Jesus reflect his own confidence in the ability and willingness of the Father to grant whatever he would ask. Jesus rebuked Peter for using the sword against those who came to arrest him and said, "Do you think that I cannot appeal to my Father, and he will at once send me more than twelve legions of angels?" (Matt. 26:53).

There can be no doubt that Jesus was the most extraordinary man of prayer the world has ever known. But is he truly an example of Christian prayer? Would it be possible for an ordinary Christian to have the same kind of power in prayer that Jesus had? It is the unhesitating answer of the New Testament that he may. Jesus himself promised: "He who believes in me will also do the works that I do; and greater works than these will he do, because I go to the Father. Whatever you ask in my name, I will do it, that the Father may be glorified in the Son" (John 14:12–13). This passage relates the promise of power in service to the promise of answered prayer "in the name of Jesus." We will consider later what that means. Here we are concerned only with the thought that the promises of Jesus open up to the ordinary believer grand vistas of power through prayer, power that matches the power which Jesus had and exercised.

Such a belief as this, of course, is based upon the Christian doctrine of the incarnation, the belief that in Jesus of Nazareth, God *really* became man. It is not within the scope of this book to discuss or seek to prove this doctrine. We must, however, take enough notice of it to convince ourselves that when Jesus prayed, he prayed for the same reason we pray—he needed to pray; and that he had open to him no resources other than those open to the believer in any age—the grace and power of God. The writer of Hebrews gives evidence of the most exalted possible opinion concerning the deity, the true Godhood, of Jesus, saying, "He reflects the glory of God and bears the very stamp of his nature, upholding the universe by his word of power" (Heb. 1:3). At the same time, the writer expresses in the clearest possible way the true humanity of Jesus, saying: "Therefore he had to be made like his brethren in every respect, so that he might become a merciful and faithful high priest in the service of God, to make expiation for the sins of the people. For because he himself has suffered and been tempted, he is able to help those who are tempted" (Heb. 2:17–18); "we have not a high priest who is unable to sympathize with our weaknesses, but one who in every respect has been tempted as we are, yet without sinning" (Heb. 4:15); and "in the days of his flesh, Jesus offered up prayers and supplications, with loud cries and tears, to him who was able to save him from death, and he was heard for his godly fear" (Heb. 5:7). Paul quotes an ancient Christian hymn that reflects the universal feeling of the early Christian movement concerning the pre-existent Son of God when he says, He "emptied himself, taking the form of a servant, being born in the likeness of men" (Phil. 2:7). The early Christians saw no problem in accepting the full humanity of Jesus; later Christians have had such a problem, for they have felt that to accept the full humanity of Jesus would be to deny his *full* deity. This need not follow at all; we must accept the incarnation as a mystery that can never be understood but is a fact nonetheless.

For our subject it is important to understand that Jesus did not go through the motions of prayer; he did not pray merely as an example. He really prayed. He prayed because prayer was to him the breath of life, the fountain of all knowledge, the source of all power, and the meaning of all existence. He prayed because he needed the help and power of the Father. He addressed himself to his Father, but his Father is our Father too. He had prayer power, not because he was the Divine One, but because he was the perfect human one. The wide difference that exists in our approach and communion with the Father is not based upon our human nature; humanity is no hindrance to fellowship with God. Our problem is sin and failure to give full surrender to God in every circumstance of life as Jesus did. A study of his prayers should be helpful as a guide to the Christian practice of prayer.

The first of the recorded prayers of Jesus is his prayer of thanksgiving at the time he sent forth his disciples two by two. "At that time Jesus declared, 'I thank thee, Father, Lord of heaven and earth, that thou hast hidden these things from the wise and understanding and revealed them to babes; yea, Father, for such was thy gracious will.'" (Matt. 11:25–26; cf. Luke 10:21.) This prayer stands in a context that records the rejection of Jesus by the Jewish rulers, "the wise and understanding," the scribes who boasted of their knowledge of God. Yet they had not recognized Jesus or received his teachings. Only "babes," the unlearned in theological society, had received it. Perhaps this was a disappointment to Jesus; it would have been to most of us. However, he recognized it as the provision of God's sovereign will, and so gave thanks for it. Notice that this is not merely a sigh of resignation because things cannot be better, but a serene, calm acknowledgment of the propriety of God's action and will.[8] The prayer breathes the atmosphere of fellowship with God that discerns his will and sees its appropriateness, and it demonstrates the attitude of surrender and conformity to the will of God at any cost.

The second recorded prayer of Jesus is his prayer at the grave of Lazarus as he prepared to call forth the dead man. "Jesus lifted up his eyes and said, 'Father, I thank thee that thou hast heard me. I knew that thou hearest me always, but I have said this on account of the people standing by, that they may believe that thou didst send me.'" (John 11:41–42.) This prayer breathes the atmosphere of assured communion with the Father. He asks nothing of which he is uncertain; as a matter of fact, he asks nothing. He gives thanks and does it publicly, that the people may recognize the coming wonder as from the hand of God and recognize Jesus as the messenger of God. Already, he had been assured of the result. He had told his disciples before the messenger came with news of the death of Lazarus, "This illness is not unto death; it is for the glory of God, so that the Son of God may be glorified by means of it" (v. 4). His concern was that the people might know that his action was within the will of God. The true nature of prayer is revealed. Prayer "is not the setting up of the will of self, but the apprehension and taking to self of the divine will, which corresponds with the highest good of the individual."[9]

The next recorded instance of Jesus' prayer is scarcely a prayer in the accepted sense; it is more like a dialogue with the Father. It occurred when the Greeks sought to see him, and he recognized their request as the sign that "the hour has come for the Son of man to be glorified" (John 12:23; "glorified" is John's term for the experience of the cross which he recognized as the central glory of Christ). The words of Jesus in response to the request were: "Now is my soul troubled. And what shall I say? 'Father, save me from this hour'? No, for this purpose I have come to this hour. Father, glorify thy name" (vs. 27–28a). The response of the Father came in a voice from heaven that said, "I have glorified it, and I will glorify it again" (v. 28c). This prayer set the pattern for the prayers of Jesus as he faced the cross. The Gospels make no effort to camouflage the inner struggle, a struggle that began at his baptism and continued throughout his life, a struggle between the natural human shrinking from suffering and the spiritual desire of a surrendered heart to accomplish God's will at any cost. A similar struggle in many other lives has resulted in victory for the natural impulse of self-preservation. Jesus felt the force of this human impulse and cried out: "Now is my soul troubled. And what shall I say?" One thing he could have said and thought of saying was, "Father, save me from this hour." He could not have been blamed if he had sought escape. He did not; he rejected the petition for rescue, because he recognized that he had come to this hour to die. It was the will of God to save the world, and salvation demanded the death of the son. He therefore said, "Father, glorify thy name," that is, Let me suffer if I must, but be sure that thy name is glorified. The response of the Father gave him assurance and sustained him as he faced the dark hours of trial ahead.

The same spirit of submission is found in the Gethsemane prayer as recorded in the Synoptic Gospels (Mark 14:32–42;

Matt. 26:36–46; Luke 22:39–46). The hour of death was nearer now; the agony of soul as he faced the tempter was greater. Luke records that "his sweat became like great drops of blood falling down upon the ground" (Luke 22:44). The sacramental nature of his death was more evident also; he called it "this cup" (Luke 22:42, and parallels), an expression that he had already used in speaking of his coming death (cf. Mark 10:38–39). The outcome of the struggle was more undecided now; he had to repeat the prayer three times before he found courage of heart and serenity of mind to face the coming ordeal. The substance of the prayer was the same; it is found in Mark. "And going a little farther, he fell on the ground and prayed that, if it were possible, the hour might pass from him. And he said, 'Abba, Father, all things are possible to thee; remove this cup from me; yet not what I will, but what thou wilt.'" (Mark 14:35–36.) The words "if . . . possible" need explanation. There was no doubt in the mind of Jesus that this was possible in the power of God; he said, "All things are possible to thee." The only meaning that can stand here is, "if it is possible to save the world and at the same time to remove the cup from me." This was not a plea for escape at any price; this was the cry of the human Jesus shrinking from the price that he must pay. At any cost, he wanted the will of the Father to be done and he expressly said, "Yet not what I will, but what thou wilt." Here, in the agony of the Garden, we see the bright, shining light of the devotion of Jesus to his Father, his willingness to pay any price to bring the will of God to pass in the world. Though his own desire, in the struggle of the moment, might waver, his inner heart cried out that the will of the Father might be done. Again, we are not to think of this as resignation; it is a victory won in the struggle against temptation. It teaches us the object of our own prayers and the possibility that we too may win the victory over temptation no matter how strong may be our inclination in the other direction.

The so-called high-priestly prayer of Jesus (John, ch. 17) is important in our study of prayer because it reveals the heart of

Jesus, the things for which he was concerned, and it records the basis of his pleas to the Father. Because of this we have a pattern of prayer for all Christians, a pattern that may serve both in guiding the direction of our requests and as the basis on which we may hope to persuade the Father to grant them. The prayer may be divided into three parts: the petitions of Jesus for himself (vs. 1–5), the petitions for the Eleven (vs. 6–19), and the petitions for future believers (vs. 20–24). These are followed by a conclusion (vs. 25–26), that essentially reiterates the theme of v. 4.

The petitions of Jesus for himself were two: "Father, the hour has come; glorify thy Son that the Son may glorify thee" (v. 1); and, "Now, Father, glorify thou me in thy own presence with the glory which I had with thee before the world was made" (v. 5). At first glance these petitions seem to be one, but they are not. The first has reference to the cross; the second, to the exaltation of the Son after the resurrection. The first, whether it reflects the mind of Jesus or of John, viewed the cross as the true glorification of the Son. The petition was therefore a petition to let him die in such a way that it would be his true glory. The second gave expression to the confident expectation of Jesus that he would be exalted at the right hand of the Father.

The bases for these petitions are three. The plea for an answer is based first on the desire of the Son to glorify the Father (v. 1). Secondly, it is based upon the faithfulness of Jesus: "I glorified thee on earth" (v. 4a). Thirdly, it is based upon the fact that he had accomplished the work his Father had given him to do (v. 4b). Notice that the petitions were those which were the already recognized will of God for his life. His plea for an answer was grounded upon his desire that God be glorified and upon his own faithfulness in accomplishing the work of God. No wonder that Jesus could feel confident that his petitions would be granted!

The petitions of Jesus for the Eleven were three. First, "Keep them in thy name, which thou hast given me, that they may be one, even as we are one" (v. 11). The idea of the first petition is based upon two factors: (1) "The name of God" expresses all that God is and does for man; to be kept in "the name of God" is to be kept as Christians. (2) The essential nature of the Eleven as a church, as the body of Christ, demanded their unity, a unity like that of Christ with the Father, a unity that consists of a variety of persons who have found an absolute harmony of purpose and desire. The second petition was that the Father should "keep them from the evil one" (v. 15). The Greek has only "the evil," but the RSV equation with Satan is probably correct. Jesus' departure from the disciples, especially since from their viewpoint it would be a tragic and misunderstood one, would leave them vulnerable to the temptations of Satan to turn from their devotion to him. Third, Jesus asked that the Father might "sanctify them in the truth; thy word is truth" (v. 17). The implication of consecration is "not so much the selection of a man for an important work as the equipping and fitting him for its due discharge."[10] These petitions were concerned primarily with the place of the disciples in the redemptive program of God. They had to be preserved from the powerful attack of Satan; they needed to be preserved from the natural tendency toward disunity; they required spiritual equipment for the ministry. For these things, Jesus appealed to the Father, who alone could accomplish them.

The bases of his petitions for the disciples may be divided into three: the disciples belonged to God; they were facing a time of need; they had a mission to fulfill. The first appeal was made on the basis of God's ownership of the disciples. He had given them to Jesus, but they remained his; they did not belong to the world, but to God (cf. vs. 6-10). The second appeal was based on their coming need. Since the Son was leaving them, and his protecting and guiding presence would be a reality no longer, since the world would hate them for their adherence to the Son, and since the devil would attack them, they had need for divine protection and assistance (cf. vs. 11-14). Finally, their commission was mentioned. "As thou didst send me into the world, so I have sent them." (V. 18.) This is the climax of the matter. They were not merely men in need; they were divinely commissioned messengers. For their task they needed the equipment and power of the Father.

The petitions of Jesus for the future believers followed very closely the pattern of his petitions for the Eleven. The first petition was almost exactly the same: "That they may all be one; even as thou, Father, art in me, and I in thee, that they also may be in us" (v. 21). The unity here, as above, was that of the nature and purpose which harmonizes the diverse personalities of men into a unity that is divine. It was not to be an invisible, spiritual unity, but one that would be apparent to men. The second petition for future disciples was new. "Father, I desire that they also, whom thou hast given me, may be with me where I am, to behold my glory which thou hast given me in thy love for me before the foundation of the world" (v. 24). The aim of this petition is quite clear; it was for the future glorification of all Christians.

The bases of these petitions are again appropriate. The first was that the granting of them would convince the world that God had really sent the Son into the world (vs. 21–23). The second was that his protection and keeping of them would convince the world that the Father loved these future disciples (v. 23). Again, it is important to notice that Jesus took his position beside the Father and asked what the Father would naturally wish to grant. This whole prayer is a living demonstration of the principle that prayer must be for the purpose of accomplishing the will of God in human life, not for the purpose of accomplishing the human will through divine intervention.

Three prayers of Jesus from the cross are recorded in the Gospels: two by Luke, the other in parallel passages in Mark and Matthew. The first was the prayer of Jesus for the forgiveness of those who crucified him. "Father, forgive them; for they know not what they do." (Luke 23:34.) There is some uncertainty concerning the identity of those for whom he prayed. It could have been the soldiers or Pilate and the Jewish rulers—probably the latter. Their ignorance of the true nature of Jesus mitigated to some degree their guilt and made their sin forgivable. However, for our purpose, the important thing is the spirit of forgiveness and graciousness that prompted the prayer on Jesus' part. He had taught his disciples to pray for their persecutors (Matt. 5:44; Luke 6:28); now he set the example by praying for his crucifiers.

The so-called prayer of dereliction seems so out of character with Jesus that one is tempted to wonder if he actually uttered it, until we remember that there was a human soul as well as a human body suffering on the cross. Mark tells us that Jesus cried with a loud voice, "Eloi, Eloi, lama sabachthani?" and interprets the Aramaic phrase by, "My God, my God, why hast thou forsaken me?" (Mark 15:34; cf. Matt. 27:46). We may reject the supposition that God had actually forsaken Jesus at this time. Paul reminds us that "God was in Christ reconciling the world to himself" (II Cor. 5:19). At no other time in his life was Jesus more pleasing to the Father than at this moment. Only one who holds to a theory of substitution, which would make Christ actually appear as a sinner in the sight of God, would take these words as a statement of fact. It is much more likely that these words express the human consciousness of Jesus, as he suffered, suspended from the earth. Ridiculed by men, he came to feel that the Father had also forsaken him. This is a difficult passage, but it would seem that we must take it simply as an expression of the depth of agony, both physical and spiritual, which Jesus endured for our sake on the cross.

What doubts might exist about the faith and confidence of Jesus in his Father are dispelled by his last earthly prayer. "Then Jesus, crying with a loud voice, said, 'Father, into thy hands I commit my spirit!'" (Luke 23:46.) This prayer, again couched in the words of the psalmist (cf. 31:5), shows the mind of Jesus soaring above his doubts and despair to the plane of simple confidence and trust in the Father. No other saying of Jesus so aptly illustrates the true spirit of the man of faith in the extremity of pain and death.

In closing our discussion of the prayer life of Jesus, let us summarize some of the principles of prayer that are illustrated by his practice. The first of these is certainly that prayer for the man of

God should not be an occasional call to the Father from the depths of despair and need; it should, on the contrary, be a constant and continuing fellowship with God in all the ways of life. It is true that God listens to the cry of despair; it is more true that God is pleased with the constant communion of his children. Jesus exemplified the practice of communion with God to the highest degree. His consciousness of the presence of the Father was a constant and vital element in all of his thought. He believed that his work was a demonstration of the dynamic presence of God (John 5:17). He insisted that even his words were not spoken on his own authority but were evidence of the indwelling work of the Father (John 14:10). His whole life was bathed in the presence of his Father. In this he sets the supreme example of his own teaching that men "ought always to pray and not lose heart" (Luke 18:1). His practice of communion with the Father shows how it is possible for us to follow the admonition of Paul and "pray constantly" (I Thess. 5:17). True, we have noticed that Jesus practiced withdrawal into quiet places for the purpose of periods of prayer, that he sometimes spent the whole night in prayer. But these periods of special prayer did not break into the routine of a godless life; they were the natural outgrowth of a life lived in communion with God.

Secondly, we notice that the prayer life of Jesus demonstrated his constant dependence on the guidance of God. In every great event and turning point in his ministry, prayer played a vital part. He did not choose the Twelve without the guidance of the Father (Luke 6:12); he dared not challenge the faith of the disciples without seeking the will of the Father in prayer (Luke 9:18). His motto of life is expressed in the words: "I seek not my own will but the will of him who sent me" (John 5:30). But if a life is to fulfill the will and desire of God, it must seek the guidance of God. Otherwise, how will we know what God's will is? This emphasizes one of the often neglected elements in prayer, the element of listening. Prayer ought to be a two-way intercourse in which we not only speak to God about our problems but also permit God to speak to us about our lives. Jesus seemed never to be in doubt about the will of God for him; we often are. Is the reason to be found in our failure to pray as we ought to pray?

Thirdly, Jesus exemplified in his prayer life the quality of absolute self-committal to the Father. His prayer was never selfish because he was never selfish. In all his prayers we find not a single request that could be interpreted as a selfish request. Although he taught that we might pray for personal benefits, protection, and help, we never find that he did so. Perhaps one reason our prayer life is so fruitless is that it consists in the main of requests for those things which we may spend in satisfying our own desires (cf. James 4:3). This self-committal of Jesus is most clearly seen in his prayers as he faced the cross and realized the dread agony that was to be his. Though he shrank from the thought, he never, as we have seen, wavered from his desire to accomplish the will of God through his life. It is no wonder that men had confidence in him as a man of prayer; it is no wonder that he had an unwavering confidence that God would hear and answer his prayers even if it involved the calling for twelve legions of angels to rescue him.

Finally, the prayer life of Jesus shows an unwavering confidence in God's love, power, and wisdom. Perhaps we have said this above; at least we have implied it; however, it needs to be stressed. To have confidence in the love of God is to believe that whatever God wills is ultimately for our benefit. To have confidence in his power is to believe that nothing is beyond his ability to help. To have confidence in his wisdom is to believe that what God chooses is always the best choice. Prayer communion with God must be built upon the solid foundation of such complete confidence in God as is evident at every point in the life and ministry of Jesus.

The Model Prayer—Synopsis

The model prayer came as Jesus' response to a request by his disciples that he teach them how to pray.

The two accounts of the prayer are basically in harmony, though they contain important variations.

The prayer is only relatively original.

Its intended purpose was to help Christians learn to pray.

Each petition is a challenge to action as well as a cry to God for help.

The order of petitions points to the proper concerns of the Christian.

The address and each of the six petitions give us important insight into the nature of prayer and summarize the petitions that are proper to present to God.

The prayer illustrates the following principles of Christian prayer: brevity, simplicity, universality, childlikeness, commitment, and humility.

III

The Model Prayer

The Master is praying again."

"What is so unusual about that? He is always praying."

"I know. He has a communion with God that surpasses anything I have ever seen in other men."

"That's true. I wish I could pray like he does."

"Perhaps we can. Let's ask him to teach us to pray."

This imaginary conversation between two of the disciples of Jesus may well have been the occasion for one of the greatest, if not the greatest, teachings on prayer that the world has ever known. Luke tells us that the model prayer (often, but erroneously, called the Lord's Prayer) was given in response to the request of Jesus' disciples that he teach them to pray.

This little prayer, so brief, so superb, is one of the greatest treasures of the Christian community throughout the world. Known better, perhaps, than any other passage of Scripture, used more widely, perhaps, than any other prayer in Christian worship, it stands in our literature and heritage as an instruction in the basic principles of prayer and as a challenge to scale the heights of the most exalted practice of prayer. Like so much of our Lord's teaching, this prayer is so simple that even a child can follow it, and so exalted that even the greatest saint must fall short of its full attainment. Some have called it "the school of prayer." Indeed, it is a school, but unlike all other schools, it is both a kindergarten and a university.

It needs to be practiced, not discussed. Yet it needs to be discussed in order that it may be practiced. Some of its language, though clear to men of old, is strange to modern ears. Some of its petitions, though apparently so simple that a child would be able to understand, give the most learned scholars difficulty.

Discussion, we trust, will lead to understanding and challenge to practice. We must consider, first, some general questions about the prayer as a whole; then we should look carefully at each particular petition and make sure that we understand all that is involved in each one; finally, we can summarize the basic principles of prayer that are illustrated by this prayer.

First, there is the question of the two accounts of the prayer, one in Luke (Luke 11:1–4), the other in Matthew (Matt. 6:9–13). A comparison shows that they exhibit a fundamental unity, but contain important variations. They are alike in the address and in five of the petitions; they differ in the reported occasion of the prayer, in the wording of the address and the common petitions, and in the addition of one petition by Matthew and the expansion of another. It is probable, if we assume that the prayer was given on only one occasion by Jesus (an assumption that is by no means certain), that the setting of the prayer in Luke is the correct one. Luke tells us that the request of the disciples came at the close of one of Jesus' own seasons of prayer. What more is natural than to suppose that the disciples, impressed by the prayer communion of Jesus with the Father, asked him to teach them to pray in the same way? Matthew includes the prayer in the central portion of the Sermon on the Mount as an example of how men can avoid the errors of Pharisees and pagans in their praying. Since Matthew is well known for grouping the teachings of Jesus on similar subjects without regard for the original setting, it is likely that he has done the same thing here.

When the wording of the two accounts is compared, we find that it is not so much a matter of difference, but a matter of expansion on the part of Matthew. "Father" is expanded to "Our Father who art in heaven." The first half of the prayer is expanded to include "Thy will be done, On earth as it is in heaven." The last petition is expanded by adding "But deliver us from evil." The tense of the verb in the saying "As we also have forgiven our debtors" is changed from the present, as it is in Luke, to the aorist tense. Finally, "debts" is substituted for "sins" in Matthew's account and thus reads: "Forgive us our debts."

The explanations of these variations may lie in several directions. First, some of the additions seem merely to be explanations in Matthew of terms in Luke that cry out for expansion, explanations that clarify the meaning of the Master rather than change the prayer. It is suggested that the phrase "who art in heaven" added to the simple address "Father" "saved the word from our humanness."[11] It could well be that the simple address of "Father" would lead to an irreverent intimacy which might need to be corrected. We will notice below that the addition of the expression "But deliver us from evil" gives the probable clue to the meaning of the petition "Lead us not into temptation." Second, it is possible that we have different translations of the Aramaic in which the prayer came from the lips of Jesus. This would explain the variation in tense, since no similar distinction existed in Aramaic. It would also seem to be the real reason for the confusion over the meaning of the Greek word *epiousion* in the petition for daily bread. Third, the fact that Matthew and Luke wrote for different audiences might explain Matthew's substitution of the Jewish term "debts" for Luke's term "sins." In this case, however, it might be that Luke is the one who changed the wording. Jesus would have been more likely, in the original setting of the prayer, to have used the Jewish term rather than the Christian term for sin.

Some have suggested that the variations may be due in large measure to the fact that Matthew sought to adapt the prayer to liturgical use. I doubt the validity of this explanation. True, Matthew's account presents a more balanced prayer and is more readily adaptable to liturgical use. This is apparent from the fact that the doxology (found in later texts, but not in the primitive texts) was attached to Matthew's version of the prayer and never to Luke's. However, there is no evidence that liturgical practice in Christian communities began as early as the first century. It did begin early in Christian history, but probably not that early. This is supported by the fact that the liturgical addition to the prayer is found among the ancient Greek and Latin commentators

only in Chrysostom (a teacher of the fifth century) and his followers. It does not appear in any text of the New Testament
which is dated that early. When liturgical use of the prayer began,
it is likely that Matthew's account was chosen because it was
adaptable, and it is unlikely that Matthew consciously sought to
make the prayer liturgical.

We need not spend much time in discussing the originality of
the prayer. It is possible by diligent search to find almost exact
parallels to each of the six petitions in some Jewish source. The
originality of the prayer lies in the fact that Jesus, whether consciously using widely scattered Jewish sources or not, has composed a prayer of tremendous beauty, which has served as the
pattern of Christian prayer for twenty centuries and will continue
to do so until the end of time. Strikingly different from all Jewish
prayers are the brevity, the order, and the universality of the
prayer. In six short petitions (if we adopt Matthew's version),
putting first things first, the prayer drives to the heart of the universal needs of all mankind.[12]

The intended use of the prayer in Christian devotion need de-
tain us only shortly. Introduced in Matthew by the expression
"Pray then like this" and reported in Luke as the Lord's response
to the request "Lord, teach us to pray," there can be little doubt
that this is a pattern rather than a formula of prayer. It, of course,
can be used as a formula and has been so used with meaning,
though not always. But its primary value lies in the pattern it sets
which enables every Christian to pray creatively as he faces the
needs of life. Here we find the proper petitions that may be addressed to God, the order of concern that should engross the
Christian's mind, the basis on which we can pray for that which
seems to be selfish, and the spirit of devotion exemplified, which
makes it possible to pray at all.

One question engaging our attention is the relation of the
prayer to Christian action. Is the prayer a call to God for help,
or is it a petition for God to act alone? Lohmeyer[13] argues that
the first petition is a prayer for the eschatological action of God.
He rejects the interpretation of Augustine and Luther, who
thought the petition was for the name of God to be hallowed by

men. He points out that to interpret the petition in this way makes it a task as well as a petition, a task that is ever incomplete and demands the constant action of the worshiper. Basing his conclusion on the aorist form of the imperative, which he interprets as restricting the action to a once-for-all action, he supports his thesis by supposing that the passive mood is a disguise for the action of God and believes also that a petition to God is proper only if it envisions fulfillment by the act of God alone.

What Lohmeyer says about the first petition might be said with equal force about the first three petitions. However, I must differ from his conclusions and accept the interpretation of Augustine and Luther for the following reasons:

1. The aorist form in the imperative mood does not necessarily imply a once-for-all act. It is true that grammarians usually say that the action indicated by the aorist tense is punctiliar, but this does not necessarily mean that the action takes place in a point of time. It would be perfectly proper to use the aorist to say, "He ate bread all the days of his life." This statement would mean that a number of individual acts of a man viewed as a whole and the aorist was used because of this perspective. The same may be true in relation to the petitions before us. The whole of life may be thought of as a quest for the hallowing of the name of God, the experiencing of God's rule, and the doing of God's will. Lohmeyer's fundamental argument loses its force when the true nature of the aorist tense in Greek is considered.

2. There is nothing inconsistent in asking God to do something that calls for the attendant action of men. We ask for bread, but we must work. We ask for deliverance from evil, but we must struggle. The reason that we ask God to do what it is our duty to do is not to escape the responsibility and necessity of action, but to ensure the success of action. God does not usually do things *for* us, but *through* us. Therefore it is perfectly consistent for us to ask God to hallow his name, to bring in his Kingdom, and to see that his will is done, even though each of these represents an unending task of our own lives.

3. Finally, it is more consistent with the prayer as a whole to think of each petition as representing a daily need; certainly the

second portion deals with needs that are constant. This is not a prayer to be prayed once and for all; it is a model of the Christian's daily prayer and devotion.

A word needs to be said about the order of the petitions in the prayer. They are six in number, composed of two groups of three. The first group, in harmony with the Ten Commandments, is concerned with things that affect the rule of God in the world. The petitions center around the pronoun "thy"—"thy name," "thy kingdom," "thy will." The second group of petitions centers around the needs of the Christian life in its everyday concerns—"Give us," "Forgive us," and "Lead us not." The order of the petitions suggests the order of the concerns that should be characteristic of the Christian, which must be characteristic of the Christian before he can truly pray. Our chief concern must be with those world affairs which concern and affect the rule of God in the world; our subsidiary concern must be for our own everyday needs, needs that must be met before we can take our place under God's redemptive rule. They are therefore a proper concern of the Father's as they are of ours. "It is only as man recognizes the supremacy of God's will and sovereignty over his life, that man may pray for anything. But having duly recognized that will and that sovereignty, he may pray for all his individual and social needs."[14]

The suggested address of the prayer is: "Our Father who art in heaven." The intimacy of the child, the unity of the Christian community, and the reverence of the worshiper are all contained in this simple address. The idea of the Fatherhood of God received new and significant meaning through the ministry of Jesus Christ. It is true that Israel had spoken of God as the father of the people, sometimes even as the father of the individual Israelite. True also is it that we have a few instances of a Jew addressing God as "my father." It is true also that other religions often spoke of their deity as father.[15] But nowhere in Jewish or pagan practice or literature do we find that fatherhood is made the regulative and basic idea in thinking of God as it was in the life and teaching of Jesus. His own consciousness of a unique Sonship led him to think of religious relationships in family terms and to use the term "Father" with a profound and loving intimacy. This privilege of direct and intimate approach to God as Father, Jesus extended to all believers when he commanded Mary to go and tell "my brethren . . . , I am ascending to my Father and your Father, to my God and your God" (John 20:17). Thus he inducted all believers into the family of God and opened the way for our approach to God, not as strangers but as children. What Jesus did in his ministry, the Spirit of God continues to do in his. "For you did not receive the spirit of slavery to fall back into fear, but you have received the spirit of sonship. When we cry, 'Abba! Father!' it is the Spirit himself bearing witness with our spirit that we are children of God" (Rom. 8:15–16). There is nothing more wonderful nor more Christian than the privilege of approaching God as Father.

Privilege may be abused; familiarity may lead to irreverence. Whether this fact caused Matthew's expansion of Luke's simple "Father" into "Our Father who art in heaven" or not, it is a true Christian addition and reflects the mind of Christ. There is never, in the New Testament, any suggestion of a lack of reverence for God. The expression "who art in heaven" is a common Jewish expression found occasionally in prayers but usually in the teachings of the rabbis. To the Jewish mind, it represented God as being unattainably exalted and stood as a barrier to fellowship with him. Such is not the intention of it in this prayer. Using the phrase in Christian prayer guards the Christian's heart against irreverence: God remains God to him even though he is also Father.

The plural pronoun "our" as used in the prayer is not a sign that the prayer was used only by groups; it is a reminder that the individual Christian does not exist in isolation from other Christians. He is a member of the "household of God" (Eph. 2:19), where there "cannot be Greek and Jew, circumcised and uncircumcised, barbarian, Scythian, slave, free man, but Christ is all, and in all" (Col. 3:11). To pray "Our Father" is to have a sense of unity with all Christians and to take up unto ourselves the problems of all the Christian community.

This address sets the pattern for all prayer in the New Testa-

ment. We sometimes hear prayers addressed to Jesus or to the
Holy Spirit, especially among the more enthusiastic Christian
groups. Even some of our hymns are composed in the form of
prayers to Christ or the Holy Spirit, hymns that are often stately
in movement and beautiful in sentiment. This seems to be a
deviation from the pattern of the New Testament. Prayer is always addressed to the Father; it may be addressed "in the name"
of Jesus; it may call for the sending of the Holy Spirit; but it is
always addressed to God as our Father and the Father of our
Lord Jesus Christ. This may be thought a small matter; perhaps
it is. However, it would seem wise to avoid this deviation if we
hope to be true to the pattern of prayer that is indicated in the
New Testament.

The first petition is: "Hallowed be thy name." "The name" of
God plays an important role in Biblical thought; it is the hidden
center of Old Testament revelation. "The name is simply the
revelation of God as a Person. . . . The 'name' means: God himself is the one who makes himself known. . . . Thus in the 'name'
there is a wonderful union of holiness, as the self-affirmation of
God, and mercy, as the self-giving of God."[16] An attitude toward
the name of God is therefore an attitude toward God. There is
nothing more basic in religion than this; to pray for the right
attitude toward God to prevail is properly the first concern of
Christian prayer.

What does it mean to "hallow" the "name" of God? This is
one of the words of the prayer, quite familiar in Biblical times,
which is strange to our modern ears. The basic meaning of the
verb "hallow" (Greek, *hagiazō*) is that of separation. In the Old
Testament it was often used for setting aside things, animals, and
buildings for the exclusive use of God. A thing was holy because
it belonged to God. In the New Testament, the word took on more
personal and moral characteristics. Salvation becomes the "hallowing," the "consecration," of the individual by God to himself.
Every Christian becomes a "saint" because he belongs to God.

Perhaps the best commentary on this petition is the first four
commandments: "You shall have no other gods before me. You
shall not make for yourself a graven image. . . . You shall not

take the name of the Lord your God in vain. . . . Remember the sabbath day, to keep it holy" (Ex. 20:3–8). The purpose of these commandments was to guard Israel against the temptation to make "God" a common noun rather than a proper noun.

The purpose of this petition in the model prayer is to guard the Christian against the same temptation. A New Testament example of the meaning of "hallow" is: "But in your hearts reverence Christ as Lord" (I Peter 3:15). The same Greek word is used in Peter as in our petition, but it has been correctly translated by "reverence" in RSV. To "hallow" the name of God would certainly mean that we would have a feeling of reverence and awe before him and that we would avoid all profanity and irreverent speech. But it would mean more; it would mean "to respond to God with reverent worship, grateful faith, and humble acceptance of his claim and promise."[17]

What does it mean to pray for the "hallowing" of the name of our Father? We have already discussed and rejected the idea that this is a prayer for the eschatological action of God in making his name "holy" over all the world. It is a prayer that God will enable me to "hallow" his name in my thought of him, in my daily conduct, and in my worship. Before I can pray for more, I must pray for this. Before I can pray for more, I must somehow achieve this proper attitude of heart and mind. This is why I must pray this prayer. I cannot "hallow" the name of God by myself. "The carnal mind . . . is not subject to the law of God, neither indeed can be." (Rom. 8:7, KJV.) But once I have prayed for this, once I have, through God's grace, begun to achieve this, I must pray for more. I cannot be satisfied to be a lone worshiper; I must long for all the world to share the "secret of glory" with me. So to the simple petition as we have it in the Bible, I must add, "Hallowed be thy name in me, through me, in the world and by the world." This petition is both personal and universal. It demands the spirit of the missionary as well as the spirit of the worshiper. It begins with me, but if it stops with me, it never really began; it must widen out in ever-increasing scope until it includes all men.

This dual nature of personal-universal request is true of each

of the first three petitions. A prayer for the Kingdom to come is
a prayer for it to come in me and through me to all the world;
a prayer for God's will to be done is a prayer for it to be done
in me, by me, and in all the world. These are no easygoing
petitions, no pious platitudes; they are both petition and challenge.
One cannot pray them as Jesus meant them to be prayed unless he
is ready to become involved as a participant in God's redemptive
purpose in the world.

The second petition is: "Thy kingdom come." How strange is
this petition to our ears! We speak of "kings" as if they were
rogues. We speak of the United Kingdom as a political realm
over which successive "kings or queens" rule. The meaning of the
term "kingdom" has been lost. In New Testament times, kingdom
meant the rule or reign of a person; the king was the symbol of
ultimate power and authority in the realm of human affairs. It
was natural for religious men to think of their deity as a king.
To pray for the coming of the Kingdom of God was considered
an essential element of prayer by the Jews: "Every pious Jew
in our Lord's day prayed in the words of the *Kaddish,* 'May his
kingdom be established in your lifetime.' "[18]

The central affirmation of Jesus in his preaching was that
"the kingdom of God is at hand" (Mark 1:15). Jesus, in answering the accusation that he wrought miracles by the power of
Satan, said, "If it is by the Spirit of God that I cast out demons,
then the kingdom of God has come upon you" (Matt. 12:28).
Jesus believed that his ministry was the turning point in the
establishment of the authority and sovereignty of God over men.
True, God has always reigned insofar as power reigns. From the
beginning, he is creator and sovereign over the universe. But
God's desire is that he might reign in the hearts of men, that men
might be voluntarily subject to him. This kind of authority is
different from that of earthly rulers. It is the authority of love
and redemption.

It is the Kingdom of God in this sense that is the subject of
the teaching of Jesus and the object of our prayer. Jesus established this spiritual reign of God through his ministry. He

opened the way for all men to come under the sway of God's love and thus to enjoy the blessings of the future world. But the ministry of Jesus is incomplete until every heart has voluntarily submitted to the rule of God. Our prayer is a prayer for the expansion of that rule. Perhaps there are four senses in which the Kingdom "comes" into the lives of men. (1) The Kingdom comes when an individual accepts God's rule over his own life through a personal surrender to the Lordship of Christ. (2) The Kingdom comes in the corporate life of a church when that church becomes in reality a "body of Christ," an instrument for achieving God's will in history. (3) The Kingdom comes in society as and to the degree that society is transformed into a life of love and concern for others and is thus made correspondingly less a reign of evil. (4) The Kingdom comes at the end of history when Christ "delivers the kingdom to God the Father after destroying every rule and every authority and power" (I Cor. 15:24) and God has become in reality "everything to every one" (v. 28).[19]

The third petition is: "Thy will be done." The will of God in this petition is to be interpreted as the desire of God, what God wants. "It is health, not disease; purity, not lust; service, not selfishness; giving, not grabbing; love and not hate; the Golden Rule and not the rule of the jungle."[20] It is important that we notice that the will of God is a positive reality rather than a negative one. Men have been inclined to think of the will of God as identified with suffering and sorrow. We have tended to make the petition "Thy will be done" a pious sigh of resignation rather than a battle cry.[21]

"On earth as it is in heaven" may be attached to all three of these petitions, or it may apply only to the last. In any case, the standard of measurement is heaven, and in heaven the name of God is completely and consistently hallowed, the rule of God is completely established, and will of God is perfectly done. Our petitions here may not stop until they have all been finally realized on earth to the degree that they are practiced in heaven.

The fourth petition is: "Give us this day our daily bread"

(Matt. 6:11). Luke substitutes "each day" for "this day" (Luke 11:3). There is much difference of opinion among scholars as to the meaning of "our daily bread" (Greek, *epiousion*). Four possibilities exist, but since the word is not found in secular Greek except for a single papyrus, the exact meaning may not be recoverable. The four possibilities are: (1) Bread necessary for life, (2) bread that is steadfast and faithful, (3) bread for the day in question, and (4) bread for the morrow.[22] Johnson limits the possibilities to the last two as the most likely, and this agrees with the conclusion of Bowman and Tapp that the word represents an unsuccessful attempt to translate the underlying Aramaic which really means "day by day."[23] There seems to be little doubt, therefore, that the common English translation gives a valid meaning of the term, and this is further indicated by the additions of the adverbial expressions "today" (Matthew) and "day by day" (Luke). This petition reminds us of our constant dependence on God for the necessities of life and teaches us that there is no way for trust to operate except on a day-by-day basis. We do not demand of God that he provide for our whole future; we only ask that he provide for each day as it arrives.

The meaning of "bread" has been debated, stemming primarily from a misconception of the earthiness of the Christian religion. Some interpreters have supposed that the petition for the daily "stuff" of life is too crass and earthy for a spiritual man and have supposed that the bread of the prayer is either "spiritual" bread or "sacramental" bread.[24] However, there is no need to "spiritualize" this petition in spite of the fact that we find no instance in the New Testament of men actually praying this prayer. No doubt the reason for this is that no instance is recorded in which it would have been proper to record the prayer. There is, as Hunter puts it, a "holy materialism" in Christianity, and Jesus enjoined the disciples to lay aside worry about material things, with the assertion, "Your heavenly Father knows that you need them all"—i.e., food and clothing and shelter (cf. Matt. 6:32). He promised that God would add these things to us if we seek above all else "his kingdom and his righteousness" (v. 33).

How much is involved in the "bread" of life is variously interpreted. The expression must be interpreted against the Oriental background of "breaking bread," which might involve a mere crust of bread in time of famine or a luxurious meal in time of plenty. One writer has suggested that it is "daily bread, not daily cake."[25] Another has objected that "God does not keep his people on a starvation diet!"[26] Luther's Small Catechism contains a famous list of things that "bread" means: food, drink, clothes, shoes, houses, farms, fields, lands, money, property, a good marriage, good children, honest and faithful public servants, a just government, favorable weather (neither too hot nor too cold!), health, honors, good friends, loyal neighbors.[27] Perhaps the best commentary on the meaning of the term in the prayer is in the discourse of Jesus on the folly of worry (Matt. 6:19–34). The things that the heathen seek and that Christians are inclined to worry about are food, drink, clothing, and shelter. These are the necessities of life. The petition suggests that the provision of these things must be entrusted by the Christian into the hands of his Heavenly Father, so that his mind and heart may be centered in seeking the Kingdom of God.

One thing might need mention. "Give us" does not invite idleness. The fact that the daily necessities of life are the gifts of God does not rule out the use of human effort, forethought, and planning. It merely recognizes that human effort and wisdom are not enough in themselves to provide even the material things of life; divine help is needed. Divine help is promised by Jesus. Christians are encouraged to bring their petitions in relation to the earthly necessities of life to the throne of God.

The fifth petition is: "Forgive us our debts, As we also have forgiven our debtors" (Matt. 6:12). Luke's account changes debts to "sins" and the "have forgiven" (Greek, *aorist*) to the present tense (Luke 11:4a). The probable reason for the change is to be found in the fact that Matthew's Gospel was addressed primarily to Jewish people, who considered that perfect righteousness was an obligation that men owed to God; thus any deviation from righteousness involved a man in a "debt" to God. Luke, on the other hand, was probably addressed to Gentile Christians to whom the term "sin" (literally, falling short) was the accepted term for a deviation from the desire and will of God. The two words come to the same thing. Christians are commanded to be righteous; God provides for the possibility that we may overcome our temptations and be righteous. However, no Christian has ever achieved perfect righteousness. On the contrary, we sin. The wonderful grace of God permits us to ask for and receive forgiveness of our sins so that our continuing fellowship with him may be a living reality. John reminds us that "If we confess our sins, he is faithful and just, and will forgive our sins and cleanse us from all unrighteousness" (I John 1:9). This seems, at first glance, to be a contradiction; we would expect John to say that God's forgiveness would arise out of his love and pity, not out of his truth and justice. However, when we recognize that the forgiveness of recognized and confessed sin is a part of the disciplinary program of God for the maturing of our character, we see the reason for John's choice of terms. Because the character of God is faithful and just, we may pray this prayer with confidence.

The second clause of this petition: "As we also have forgiven our debtors," seems to be, until further consideration is given to it, an attempt to buy our own forgiveness by forgiving. First, let it be noticed that the act of forgiving is not really said to precede the reception of forgiveness; neither the Greek nor the Aramaic will stand this interpretation.[28] The real explanation of this addition to the petition and the emphasis upon it in the assertion of Jesus that our forgiveness is impossible unless we forgive men (Matt. 6:14–15) lies in another direction. It rests upon an essential element of human nature. Hatred and resentment, as long as they are harbored in the heart of man, shut out all that is loving and gentle and good—in a word, they shut God out. "God cannot enter the frozen heart of him who hates."[29] "Unforgiving" must always be "unforgiven" for this reason. Forgiveness involves much more than the remission of the penalty of wrong; it involves the reestablishment of fellowship. The forgiven sin may not be forgotten, but God does not hold the sin to the account of the sinner. Fellowship is a two-way road; it demands the proper attitude of heart on the part of the one forgiven just as much as on the part of the pardoner. Because of this, our forgiveness of others is a necessary attendant circumstance in our being forgiven of God.

The last petition of the model prayer is: "Lead us not into temptation, But deliver us from evil" (Matt. 6:13). The second half of this petition is not contained in Luke's account of the prayer. The petition creates some difficulty in the light of the assertion of James, "Let no one say when he is tempted, 'I am tempted by God'; for God cannot be tempted with evil and he himself tempts no one; but each person is tempted when he is lured and enticed by his own desire" (James 1:13-14). Why should we ask God not to do something that he does not do at all? One possible solution is to recognize that the Greek word for "temptation" (*peirasmon*) can also mean trials or testing experiences. In this respect, it is possible to think of God's leading us into temptations. It is recorded that after his baptism, "Jesus was led up by the Spirit into the wilderness to be tempted by the devil" (Matt. 4:1). Testing and trials are necessary to growth; this is seen in the realm of nature as well as in human life. But why should one pray to his Heavenly Father to be preserved from the very thing that will ensure his spiritual growth? Is it because he naturally shrinks from the idea of testing? This might be an adequate explanation if we were concerned only with human desire. What we have in this prayer, however, is a pattern divinely given for our prayer life. It is not likely that the Father would command us to pray for exclusion from those experiences of life which he finds necessary for our growth.

Perhaps the answer is found in Matthew's addition which, if not a part of the original prayer, is at least the first attempt at interpreting the mind of Christ in this petition: "But deliver us from evil." If what we have is an attempt at Jewish synonymous parallelism in which the second line takes up and expands the meaning of the first, the entire petition might well be understood to mean: "Do not let us be overcome by temptation, but deliver us from evil." If such a meaning could be assumed, the parallelism would be perfect and the petition would then become perfectly natural and necessary, complementing the prayer for forgiveness in the former petition. Unfortunately, there is no philological evidence that would permit the translation of the Greek verb in this way. This solution must remain conjecture, but it is to be preferred to what seems to be the plain meaning of the text, a meaning which, if "temptation" be taken as seduction to evil, is unnecessary and which, if "temptation" be taken as trials, seems unworthy of the Christian heart.[30]

Some of the most basic principles of Christian prayer are illustrated by this prayer. First, we note its brevity. Here we have no holy loquacity, no reading of a news bulletin on earth's affairs to heaven. The "empty babbling" of the pagan prayer is avoided. We must remember that prayer is never effective because it is long; there is no need of tiring out God with our "much speaking." Second, we note the simplicity of the petitions. With sharp, arrowlike swiftness they drive to the heart of the desire and need of the worshiper. The man who hesitates to pray because he does not know what to say would do well to make this prayer the pattern of his petitions. Third, we note the universality of the petitions. These are things that concern man at the deepest level of his existence. Fourth, we notice the childlikeness of the prayer. One who prays thus must learn to trust his Father as the earthly child trusts his earthly father. Fifth, there is the spirit of commitment, of dedication, which underlies this prayer. It is the prayer not of the spectator but of the participant. It is the prayer of one who has made God's cause his cause and cries out for help to play his part well in God's redemptive rule. Sixth, there is the spirit of humility, the recognition of man's dependence upon God for the necessities of life. The proud man cannot pray this prayer. He who feels himself to be self-sufficient cannot pray thus. It is only as we recognize the fundamental weakness of our own lives and realize that the accomplishment of any good must be gained with the help of God that we can pray this prayer.

Thanksgiving—Synopsis

Prayer can be thought to take many forms, depending on the personal inclination of the writer. The New Testament stresses three: thanksgiving, petition, and intercession.

Thanksgiving is based on two presuppositions: (1) all of man's blessings are gifts of God, and (2) man is unworthy of the blessings God gives.

Thanksgiving is considered to be both a Christian duty and a form of worship. This remains true in all circumstances of life. The Christian duty of thanksgiving is both individual and corporate.

We should thank God for all good gifts, but true thanksgiving delights to enumerate the gifts of God.

We should be thankful for the material blessings of life. The prayer of thanksgiving has the effect of consecrating our common meals.

Prayers of thanksgiving for spiritual realities are numerous in the New Testament. Those which are enumerated are: the redemptive program of God, the blessing of salvation, the equipment for spiritual service, the reality of Christian fellowship, and the many provisions of God for our spiritual life.

One extraordinary prayer is Paul's thanksgiving that he did not baptize more of the Corinthians than he did.

IV

Forms of Prayer: Thanksgiving

Concerning the proper forms of prayer, there are many opinions. Leslie D. Weatherhead constructs a seven-room house of prayer that includes: affirmation of the presence of God, thanksgiving, confession, affirmation and reception, sincere petition, intercession for others, meditation.[31] Georgia Harkness suggests a series of moods of prayer that includes: adoration and praise, thanksgiving, confession, petition, intercession, commitment.[32] Others would limit prayer to petition alone—petition for self or for others. *"Prayer is by the very definition of the term petitionary:* what it means is asking that something we desire may take place. It is not . . . the whole of worship. Worship includes, besides prayer, acts of adoration and thanksgiving, and acts of acceptance of the Divine Will. *Prayer is just the petitionary part of worship."*[33] Without entering into debate about the limits of prayer, I have adopted the position that thanksgiving is a form of prayer and that it includes adoration and praise. Confession, I think, is simply a form of petition, or perhaps a prelude to petition for forgiveness of sins. We find no hint of meditation in the New Testament, and the limits of this book preclude any discussion of this exercise of the soul, which, when it is meditation on the grace and goodness of God, may be very beneficial. The Greek words that may be translated "meditate" (*Meletaō* and *Promeletaō*) are never used in the New Testament in this sense. Commitment is treated as a means of effective prayer rather than as a form of prayer.

In the New Testament, three forms of prayer are given a place of prominence: thanksgiving, petition, and intercession.

Judging from the number of references, thanksgiving is given the most prominent place of the three and is in one sense of the word the most Christian form of prayer, expressing, as it does, praise to God for all his goodnesses and benefits.

Undergirding the practice of thanksgiving are two fundamental presuppositions, the first of which is that all the blessings of men are the gifts of God. There is no thought in the New Testament that any man ever receives anything that is good solely as a result of his own efforts and achievement. This does not mean that man is encouraged to sit with open hands waiting for God to fill them. On the contrary, man is expected to work and labor and strive. One reason that man need not worry about the material necessities of life is that he, in contrast to the birds of the air and the grass of the field, can plan and save and work (cf. Matt. 6:26-30). This is one reason why God can be trusted to fill the needs of his children in the material realm. Man can sow and reap and gather into barns in anticipation of coming need. Nevertheless, the crops that man raises, though they may seem to be a direct result of his own labor, are the gifts of God rather than the achievement of men.

What is true in the realm of material blessings is doubly true in the realm of spiritual service. Paul stresses this fact in his letter to the Corinthians, who were inclined to give credit to the earthly ministers for their salvation and spiritual nurture. Using the figure of the field and applying it to his work and to that of Apollos, he insists that the Corinthians should think of human ministers as "servants through whom you believed, as the Lord assigned to each" (I Cor. 3:5). Figuratively speaking, Paul as the original messenger, may be said to have planted the crop, Apollos to have watered it. Their labor is not without meaning and they will each be rewarded for it, not according to the immediately apparent result, but according to their labor (v. 8). However, when the results are considered, "neither he who plants nor he who waters is anything, but only God who gives the growth" (v. 7). Paul explains his simplicity of speech in the Corinthian mission as a deliberate effort on his part to avoid any appearance of persuading the Corinthians to believe by the use of human eloquence. He was anxious that they should recognize that their faith was a "demonstration of the Spirit and power, that your faith might not rest in the wisdom of men but in the power of God" (I Cor. 2:4b-5).

The proper attitude of all people when they think of the spiritual blessings that have filled their lives is to refer them to the effective work of God and recognize that men are but the instruments of the gracious hand of the Almighty. One woman, whose husband had been led to Christ by a preacher, said to the preacher, "I thank God for letting such men as you run around loose." Crudely put though her words were, they expressed the essential truth. Her husband's conversion was not the preacher's work, it was the work of God through the preacher. Thanks were given to God, not to the preacher.

Underlying all thought of thanksgiving, then, is the necessary presupposition that all blessings, material and spiritual, are the gifts of God. But this, in itself, does not imply the necessity of thanksgiving. One other supposition must be brought to bear— the understanding that we are not worthy of any of these blessings. We have not earned them; we have not acted so as to merit them; we have not lived so as to deserve them. They are the bounties of God's grace, the gifts of God's unmerited favor, the result of his love, which bestows itself upon unworthy objects. It is at this point, more than at any other, that the modern mind is different from the New Testament mind. The New Testament writers never ceased to be amazed at the goodness of God; they never forgot that his gifts were showered upon unworthy objects. Paul marveled continually at the grace of God that came upon him. He was conscious of his unworthiness. He called himself at various times, "the least of the apostles, unfit to be called an apostle, because I persecuted the church of God" (I Cor. 15:9), "the very least of all the saints" (Eph. 3:8), and "the foremost of sinners" (I Tim. 1:15). It was this sense of absolute unworthiness that created in his heart the spontaneous outburst of thanksgiving for all the gifts of God.

Thanksgiving, in the New Testament, is considered to be both a Christian duty and a form of worship. "Through him then let us continually offer up a sacrifice of praise to God, that is, the fruit of lips that acknowledge his name." (Heb. 13:15.) The old dispensation was characterized by the variety of gifts and sacrifices that the Jews offered up to God. Christianity, because of its belief in the finality of the sacrifice of Christ, is without these material offerings but not without sacrifices, if this Scripture is to be believed. The sacrifice that is well-pleasing to God is the "fruit of our lips," our praise of God for his countless blessings.

To refuse to give thanks to God is considered to be one of the characteristic marks of men in their sin and rebellion. Paul describes the heathen as those who, although they knew God, "did not honor him as God or give thanks to him" (Rom. 1:21). By contrast, he would seem to be saying that a mark of the Christian is that he does honor God and give him thanks. Anna is said to have been a widow who "did not depart from the temple, worshiping with fasting and prayer night and day" (Luke 2:37). Among the forms of prayer that she offered to God and that were acceptable to him was the giving of thanks (v. 38).

The duty of thanksgiving for the blessings that God gives is illustrated in the story of the ten lepers who cried out to Jesus for mercy. When told to go and show themselves to the priests, they went and were cleansed on the way. One, a Samaritan, turned back to praise God and give thanks to Jesus. The disappointed remark of Jesus was: "Were not ten cleansed? Where are the nine? Was no one found to return and give praise to God except this foreigner?" (Luke 17:17–18.) Plainly implied in this statement of Jesus is the condemnation of the nine who had received the same blessing but did not return to give thanks for it. No doubt they were rejoicing in the blessing of cleansing, so much so that they forgot the source of the blessing. What a parable of the attitude of so many today who take the blessings of God as a matter of course without taking time or thought to give the credit and glory to God.

Not only does the New Testament teach the duty of thanksgiving in the time of prosperity and goodness; it also suggests that thanksgiving is a duty in time of trial and difficulty. After all, no difficulty is so great that our lives do not still contain many of the blessings of God. Often we are so engrossed in our sorrow that we forget the blessings we still have. A case in point is that of Paul and Silas in the Philippian jail; because of the accusation of the greedy and disappointed slave owners whose slave had been healed by Paul, they had been unjustly beaten, thrown into prison, and their feet fastened in stocks. Surely here was sufficient cause for grumbling and complaining. But the record is that at "midnight Paul and Silas were praying and singing hymns to God, and the prisoners were listening to them" (Acts 16:25). No doubt it was this distinctively Christian behavior, coupled with their refusal to flee when the earthquake had freed them, that led the jailer to fall down and ask, "Men, what must I do to be saved?" (v. 30).

What is taught in the New Testament was practiced by the Christians of the first century. One part of the common activity of the churches was the practice of giving thanks to God for his many blessings. It is said of the first church, following the outpouring of God's spirit and power on the Day of Pentecost, that "day by day, attending the temple together and breaking bread in their homes, they partook of food with glad and generous hearts, praising God and having favor with all the people" (Acts 2:46–47). Paul urged the Roman church to be in harmony and prayed that God might grant them grace "to live in such harmony with one another, in accord with Christ Jesus, that together you may with one voice glorify the God and Father of our Lord Jesus Christ" (Rom. 15:5–6). It is assumed that one of the duties of the church was to give praise to God and that they should seek to maintain a unity of spirit and heart, that they might, for one thing, fulfill this duty. The church at Ephesus was urged to seek a creative fellowship in its common meetings which would include mutual care and instruction and "always and for everything" to give thanks in the name of the "Lord Jesus Christ to God the Father" (Eph. 5:20). A parallel to this passage is found in the sister epistle to Colossae. "Whatever you do, in word or deed, do everything in the name of the Lord Jesus, giving thanks to God the Father through him." (Col. 3:17.) There can be no doubt that one of the important activities of every church consisted of the giving of thanks. Indeed, for a church to fail or refuse to give thanks threatened its very existence. This is illustrated by the message of the risen Christ to the church at Laodicea. Its members had come to feel that they had need of nothing, but possessed all things (cf. Rev. 3:17). No doubt such a spirit arose from their failure to recognize the fundamental assumptions of life under God and their failure to give thanks for what they had received. Jesus warned them to repent of their indifference or suffer the judgment of being spewed from his mouth (Rev. 3:15–20).

Not only does the New Testament teach that the duty of thanksgiving is a church duty to be fulfilled in the corporate life of the body of Christ, it also teaches that it is the duty and obligation of every Christian to give thanks to God. Paul admonished the Ephesians to avoid all filthiness, silly talk, and levity, which are contrary to the spirit of true Christianity, "but instead let there be thanksgiving." (Eph. 5:4.) The Philippians are given carte blanche in the things that they may ask of God, but are reminded that requests for further blessings must be accompanied by thanksgiving for past blessings if they expect God to answer (Phil. 4:6–7). The Colossian Christians are urged to abound in thanksgiving (Col. 2:7). The Thessalonians are admonished, "Give thanks in all circumstances; for this is the will of God in Christ Jesus for you" (I Thess. 5:18). It would be possible to multiply passages in which the duty and practice of thanksgiving are taught, but this is not necessary. We may take it as a settled conclusion that the living of the Christian life necessarily involves the constant giving of thanks if it is to be well-pleasing to God.

If we ask, For what shall we give thanks to God? the answer of the New Testament is "Everything" (Eph. 5:20). Of course, this would be everything that is good. Nothing that is good is to be passed over without thanksgiving, for it all comes from the bountiful hand of God. It is God who sends the rain upon the just and the unjust (Matt. 5:45); it is God who sustains the weary in his toil; it is God who blesses the fields with fruitfulness; it is God who arranges the orderliness of society; it is God who saves the sinner; it is God who sustains the tempted; it is God who gives the increase to the churches; it is God who produces the virtues of Christ in the Christian heart. All things that are good and worthwhile are from the hand of God.

However, one of the difficulties we have in our devotional life is that we give thanks to God for "all his blessings" without really giving thanks for any one of them. The particular blessings tend to become lost in the generalities of our prayer life. Our thanksgiving tends to become mere form. It will be well for us to notice some of the particular things for which the New Testament suggests that thanks be given. We should not think that the list, though it includes all the individual things that are mentioned in New Testament passages, is exhaustive. One might doubt whether such a list would be possible. As we contemplate the unsearchable riches of his grace, we are often led to burst forth with spontaneous praise according to the pattern of Paul: "O the depth of the riches and wisdom and knowledge of God! How unsearchable are his judgments and how inscrutable his ways! . . . For from him and through him and to him are all things. To him be glory for ever. Amen" (Rom. 11:33, 36). Yet such an outburst of praise is not likely unless we let our minds dwell on the particulars of God's grace and goodness.

Let us begin with what might be called the lesser blessings of life but which are nevertheless more constantly with us than any others—the material blessings. There are two of these mentioned in the New Testament, the first of which is thanksgiving for secular rulers. "First of all . . . I urge that . . . thanksgivings be made for all men, for kings and all who are in high positions, that we may lead a quiet and peaceable life, godly and respectful in every way." (I Tim. 2:1–2.) The duty of thanksgiving for political rulers, of course, rests on the total teaching of the New Testament that the man of authority is "God's servant for your good" (Rom. 13:4). According to the philosophy of the Christian community, "there is no authority except from God, and those that exist have been instituted by God" (v. 1). When we remember that the authority of which Paul spoke was the authority of the Roman Empire, presided over by the godless and unsaved, we may wonder at his willingness to identify the authority with God. Yet this authority, although it did not and could not be an instrument of grace in the preaching of the gospel, was the source of the orderly society that made the preaching of the gospel possible. In our day, when governments are far more influenced by Christian principles, the duty of thanksgiving and prayer is much greater than in the days of Paul.

The second material blessing mentioned in the New Testament is that of food and the everyday sustenance of life. Christians followed the Jewish custom of giving thanks at every meal. In doing so, they followed as well, or perhaps primarily, the custom and example of Jesus. The practice of thanksgiving is mentioned in the life of Jesus in relation to the feeding of the five thousand (cf. Matt. 14:19 and parallels), the institution of the Lord's Supper (I Cor. 11:24; Luke 22:19), and in his fellowship with the two disconsolate disciples at Emmaus (Luke 24:30). In the latter case, it was just his act of taking bread and blessing it that opened the eyes of the disciples to recognize him and that sent them back with singing hearts to assure the others that Christ was indeed alive. His giving of thanks at the institution of the Lord's Supper is the basis of calling this ordinance the Eucharist. ("Eucharist" is an Anglicized spelling of the Greek word for thanksgiving.) Some might question whether this incident belongs under the heading of thanksgiving for material benefits, and we would not argue the point. Perhaps it is true that the thanksgiving connected with the Lord's Supper should be more for what the elements stand for, the death and resurrection of Christ and the resulting salvation of men, than for the elements themselves. At any rate, we know that Jesus did make a practice of giving thanks for his food, and we should follow him at this point.

Paul did this not only in his practice but in his teaching. During the terror of the storm at sea, we are told that Paul, after a season of prayer, assured the men that God had promised safety to all men who were on the ship. "And when he had said this, he took bread, and giving thanks to God in the presence of all he broke it and began to eat." (Acts 27:35.) Paul believed and taught that the meaningful giving of thanks for food transformed the common meal into a religious meal. The giving of thanks consecrates the food, separates it to God, and makes the act of eating a sacramental one in the good sense of the word. This conception of the consecrating power of thanksgiving is found in two passages—in Paul's instruction to the Corinthians about eating meat sacrificed to idols and in his letter to Timothy.

One of the problems that plagued the church at Corinth was eating meat that had been offered by heathen worshipers to their gods, then sold in the "shambles" (the marketplace) for human consumption. Could the Christian eat it without sharing the worship of the heathen god? Paul's answer consists of a mixture of wisdom, religion, and psychology. The heathen god is nothing: yet to the weak in conscience, if he knows of the previous offering of the meat, it may constitute a threat to his single-hearted devotion to God in Christ Jesus. Each man must be his own judge at this point, and each must strive to avoid causing the other to sin. However, if the food is partaken of with thanksgiving to God, it is Paul's judgment that no guilt accrues to the one who eats and no criticism should be made of him. "If I partake with thankfulness, why am I denounced because of that for which I give thanks?" (I Cor. 10:30.) The same problem is probably in view in the letter to the Romans. "He also who eats, eats in honor of the Lord, since he gives thanks to God; while he who abstains, abstains in honor of the Lord and gives thanks to God." (Rom. 14:6.) Paul concludes his advice to the Corinthians with the general principle, "So, whether you eat or drink, or whatever you do, do all to the glory of God" (I Cor. 10:31).

More directly to the point is the passage in Timothy (I Tim. 4:3–5), which, though it may not have been written by Paul, is

Pauline in spirit and tone. Behind the passage is the contrasting attitudes toward material things in a Gnostic-inclined philosophy and in Christian teaching. The heresy that is attacked taught that all things material were evil in themselves; its teachers are characterized as those "who forbid marriage and enjoin abstinence from foods" (v. 3a). The heretics seemed to believe that the ascetic life was the only Christian life. The Christian philosophy of things, however, is that "everything created by God is good" (v. 4), that is, it is good when it is used in the way in which God meant it to be used. Therefore foods were created of God "to be received with thanksgiving by those who believe and know the truth" (v. 3b). "Nothing is to be rejected if it is received with thanksgiving; for then it is consecrated by the word of God and prayer." (Vs. 4b–5.) The idea that seems to lie behind this pronouncement is that the believer's prayer of thanksgiving transforms the common meal from an attempt to preserve human life to a religious meal that glorifies God as the giver of all good gifts.

Not because they are less important, but because they are more apparent, we may mention without so much discussion the various prayers of thanksgiving for spiritual realities. The first of these is the thanksgiving for God's redemptive program, which enables the salvation of lost men. We have already mentioned and discussed the prayer of thanksgiving by Jesus (cf. Matt. 11:25–26; Luke 10:21). The writer of The Acts records that the Gentiles glorified the word of God, the gospel of Jesus Christ, when they heard it (Acts 13:48). Paul himself shrinks with horror from any glory except that which is centered in the cross of Christ (Gal. 6:14). He thanks God for the election of the Corinthians to salvation (II Cor. 9:13) and exclaims, "Thanks be to God for his inexpressible gift!" (II Cor. 9:15). The motif of thanksgiving unto God for the many provisions of his redemptive program is carried over into the book of Revelation where the hosts of heaven are pictured as singing praises unto God for his provision of salvation for lost men (Rev. 4:9–11; 5:8–10; 11:17).

The blessing of salvation stands, as a matter of course, at the head of the list of personal spiritual blessings that men have received through the grace of God and for which they should express thanksgiving. Paul gives thanks to God that the victory over sin that he was unable to achieve in the flesh is made possible in Jesus Christ (Rom. 7:25). The church at Jerusalem overcame its racial prejudice long enough to give thanks to God that he had granted "repentance unto life" to the Gentiles (Acts 11:18). Paul gives thanks for the salvation of the Romans (Rom. 6:17) and blesses God as the one "who has blessed us in Christ with every spiritual blessing in the heavenly places" (Eph. 1:3). He urges the Colossians to give thanks to the Father, "who has qualified us to share in the inheritance of the saints in light" (Col. 1:12). Peter echoes the same note in his blessing of the Father, who has, through the resurrection of Christ, begotten us again unto a living hope (I Peter 1:3). The house of Cornelius extolled God upon receiving the Holy Spirit (Acts 10:46).

Ranking next in importance among the spiritual gifts of God are those which have to do with Christian service. Paul gives thanks to the Lord because "he judged me faithful by appointing me to his service" (I Tim. 1:12). He looked upon service to God as a high privilege, not as a burdensome duty, and thus was thankful that God permitted him to serve. He thanked God for the grace "which was given you in Christ Jesus, that in every way you were enriched in him with all speech and all knowledge . . . so that you are not lacking in any spiritual gift" (I Cor. 1:4–5, 7). Thus we see that the equipment for service is a gift from God for which thanks are due. Finally, success in service is a gift of God for which we should give thanks. Paul gives thanks to God, who causes him to triumph and spreads through him "the fragrance of the knowledge" of God everywhere (II Cor. 2:14). He expresses thanks to God for the acceptance of the word by the Thessalonians, implying that this is due to the work of God and not to the skill of the preacher (I Thess. 2:13). He even gives thanks to God for the continued growth of the Thessalonians in faith and love (II Thess. 1:3).

Next, we notice that thanksgiving is due for the reality of Christian fellowship. The Corinthians are told that Paul thanks God for putting "the same earnest care for you into the heart of Titus" (II Cor. 8:16). The Christians of Rome met Paul on his way there, and together they gave thanks to God and took courage (Acts 28:15). Paul expresses deep thanks for the continued partnership of the Philippian church in his missionary labors (Phil. 1:3–5). He thanks God for the love that the Colossians had for all the saints (Col. 1:3–4). He repeatedly assures the Thessalonians of his thankfulness for their love and fellowship (I Thess. 1:2; 3:9; II Thess. 1:3). He assured Timothy of his constant thankfulness for him whenever he remembered him in his prayers (II Tim. 1:3). He assures the Corinthians that their bounty in caring for the poor saints in Jerusalem will overflow "in many thanksgivings to God" (II Cor. 9:11–12).

The New Testament does not ignore the many personal provisions made for the Christian by a bountiful God, provisions for which God is to be thanked. It is God who gives us victory in Christ over temptation, fear, and death (I Cor. 15:57). James admonishes: "Is any cheerful? Let him sing praise" (James 5:13), thus implying that all the joys of life are to be ascribed to God. Paul blesses God for the fact that he is a God of comfort and mercies (II Cor. 1:3–4). The lame man whom Peter and John healed on the way to the temple was seen "walking and leaping and praising God" (Acts 3:8–9).

As an oddity, not as a pattern, we notice the thanksgiving of Paul (I Cor. 1:14–15) for the fact that he had personally baptized only a few of the Corinthians. The reason lies in the fact that the Corinthians were giving praise to human leaders for their spiritual blessings, and Paul feared that if he had baptized more of them, they would have some kind of superficial, though unreal, grounds for praising him instead of God for their salvation. Even in this odd expression of thanksgiving, we see shining clearly in the heart of the great apostle the conception that all good things come from God and he alone is to be thanked for them.

Petition—Synopsis

Some think petition is the only form of prayer; others think petition is sub-Christian.

The need for petition does not lie in the necessity to inform God of our needs, nor is petition a means of persuading him to meet them.

We cannot receive the best gifts of God until we consciously desire them; our need is the reason petition is necessary.

Whether we understand the need for petition or not, we are commanded to present our petitions to the Lord.

We are to pray for the needs of our everyday life. This petition illustrates the relation between our work and God's giving.

We are to pray for the necessary help to guarantee our own spiritual growth and maturity. We are told to pray for "forgiveness" and help to overcome our temptations. We are told that we may pray for wisdom.

Prayers concerning the needs of Christian service is found in the New Testament, such as prayer for spiritual gifts and prayer for the opportunity to serve.

V

Forms of Prayer: Petition

Petition means that we ask God for something that we desire to happen. There are persons who would limit prayer to this form alone; others look upon petition as sub-Christian. John R. Rice, for instance, insists that we pray only when we ask God for something. He refuses to think of thanksgiving, adoration, praise, meditation, and confession as prayer in any real sense of the word. He insists that a prayer is answered only when we receive what we have asked for in just the way we desire it.[34] I am sure that Rice goes too far, especially in characterizing prayer that does not ask for something as "hypocritical."[35] On the other hand, Rufus Jones goes too far in the other direction. He says, "Even if science could demonstrate that prayer could never effect any kind of utilitarian results, still prayer on its loftier side would remain untouched, and persons of spiritual reach would go on praying as before. If we could say nothing more, we could at least affirm that prayer, like faith, is itself the victory. The seeking is the finding. The wrestling is the blessing. It is no more a means to something else than love is. It is an end in itself. It is its own excuse for being."[36]

Perhaps the reason for such diverse opinions about the subject of petition lies, on the one hand, in a misunderstanding of why petition is necessary in order to receive the blessings of God, and on the other hand, in a misinterpretation of the New Testament teachings on what petition may accomplish. Certainly, we are not to think of God as the servant of man. Prayer is not the means of imposing our will upon God. If petition is approached in this spirit, it does become non-Christian and should be rejected. On the other hand, there is a providential reason as well as a divine command for prayer as petition.

What is the reason for petitionary prayer? Why must the Christian ask God for things? How could it be true that our asking is a necessity to the Father's giving? At first glance, it would seem that such a practice is unnecessary. It is certainly not necessary for us to petition God for what we desire in order for him to be informed of our needs. Jesus reminded his disciples, "Your Father knows what you need before you ask him" (Matt. 6:8). He warned them against anxiety over material necessities of life and assured them, "Your heavenly Father knows that you need them all" (v. 32). No, Christian prayer should never be considered to be an information service that enables heaven to know of the conditions of earth.

At the same time, it is impossible to think of petitionary prayer as a means of persuading God to do something. It is often true that we must persuade men to do what they should do; it is sometimes true that we can persuade men to do what they should not do. Neither of these things can be true of God. He does not need to be persuaded to do what he should do. He delights to give good gifts to his children. James reminds us that God "gives to all men generously and without reproaching" (James 1:5). Jesus contrasted the desire of God to give "good things" to his children with the willingness of earthly parents to give "good gifts" to their children and concluded that the Heavenly Father is *much more* ready to make such gifts than they are (Matt. 7:11). Jesus also asserted, "It is your Father's good pleasure to give you the kingdom" (Luke 12:32). The Christian can never think of his Heavenly Father as a reluctant giver who withholds his bounties until he is persuaded to yield them to anxious demands.

Nor can we think of God as one who can be persuaded to do something for us that would not be good for us or that would be inconsistent with his own character and purpose.

In one discussion of prayer, a story is told to warn against praying without taking into account the will of God. A minister's son was very ill. The minister sent telegrams to his friends and asked for their intercession. When the son did not improve, the request were repeated with even greater fervor. The son did recover, but turned out in later life to be an evil man, walking in sin and wickedness. The minister is said to have regretted his insistence on prayer for the recovery of his son. The implication of this story is that "insistent prayer" led God to grant a desire that was not within God's own will.[37] There is no justification for the conclusion reached. The facts may be accepted as true. But we may be sure that God was not persuaded by the insistent prayers of pious men to grant a blessing that turned out to be a curse. God is not that kind of God and prayer is not that kind of tool.

Even the "evil" parents of earth would not give their children a snake, nor insist that they eat a stone. An earthly parent might possibly be persuaded to grant a request of his children that he feared to be unwise for them. Their insistence might result in his yielding to their importunity. However, even the earthly parent would not yield if he knew for a certainty that the granting of the request would bring tragedy and ruin to the child. He does not always know; therefore, he sometimes yields to insistence. Not so with God. He knows not only the immediate but the ultimate outcome of all our requests. The Christian need not be concerned for a moment that he may bring about his own harm through prayer to God.

Why, then, must we ask God for things? The answer, I think, lies in the essential relation between our desire and our receiving. The New Testament never discusses this problem. Christians assumed that they should petition God for the blessings of life, and they did. God had commanded them to pray for what they wanted; to them this made petition more than a privilege: it made it a duty. We must rely for the answer on our own understanding. A moment of reflection will reveal that we never receive anything that is truly good until we desire it greatly or until that desire becomes conscious.

Accordingly, we cannot receive the best gifts of God until we become consciously aware of the fact that we need those particular gifts. One of the Beatitudes reads: "Blessed are those who hunger and thirst for righteousness, for they shall be satisfied" (Matt. 5:6). It would seem apparent that God would want to give righteousness to all men, that he would actively seek to make this gift whether man desires it or not. This is true. But righteousness cannot be given to those who are not aware of their need. Men must desire to be righteous before God can act creatively to make them so. Thus, before man can receive this "blessing," he must become conscious of his need for it, long for it with the intensity that a starving man longs for food or a thirsty man for water, and though it is not contained in his Scripture, ask God to give it to him. When this condition exists in man's heart, the way is open for God to act. Until then, God is unable to help man become righteous.

A simple illustration will clarify this relation between asking and receiving. Some years ago, when my oldest daughter was young, my wife and I decided that she should learn to play the piano. We told her that this was what she should do. We bought a piano for her to use in practice and arranged for lessons—all to no purpose. She did not want to learn; she had to be driven to practice; she was the despair of her teacher. Finally, reluctantly, we gave up, sold the piano, and decided that this was a gift we could not give to our daughter.

A few years later, she came one day with a note of pleading in her voice and asked me to give her piano lessons. My heart leaped with joy; this was what I wanted; I had only waited for her to want it. Again we bought a piano and arranged for a teacher. How different now! She practiced without urging, with only reminding; she was the joy of her teacher; she did learn to play the piano.

I think this may be the way it is between God and us. He tells us in the Scriptures what he wants us to have—a multitude of gifts. Yet we do not have them, because we have not taken God seriously and have not asked him to give them to us. William

Temple has suggested that the only reason for using words in prayer is to fix our thoughts, to redeem them from vagueness. God does not need words; but we do. God does not need to be persuaded to give us good gifts, but we need to be persuaded that we need them. When we pray, we open the door and give God access to our need.[38]

Whether we understand the reason for petition or not, we must certainly understand that we are commanded to pray in this way. Martin Luther made much of this fact; he believed that the command to pray was all that was needed on our part. Jesus said, "Keep on asking and it shall be given to you" (Matt. 7:7, my translation). The Greek present tense in this verse may be interpreted to mean that we are to keep on habitually presenting our various petitions as they arise and God will keep on giving to us the things we need. We are promised that whatever we ask in prayer, we will receive, if we have faith (Matt. 21:22). James reminds his readers, "You do not have, because you do not ask" (James 4:2). The writer of I Timothy says, "I urge that supplications, prayers, intercessions, and thanksgivings be made for all men" (I Tim. 2:1). The Greek word that is here translated "urged" has various degrees of force. It may, at times, be translated by "I exhort" or "I beseech," and even by "I command." There is no doubt that the writer felt that prayer was a Christian duty which should be urged upon all Christians.

Paul also makes prayer in the form of petition a command. "Have no anxiety about anything, but in everything by prayer and supplication with thanksgiving let your requests be made known to God." (Phil. 4:6.) Perhaps the reason that so many modern Christians have not found the cure for anxiety is that they have sought it in the wrong way. The Scriptural way is through prayer. As we face the various circumstances, problems, burdens, and obstacles of life, we are invited—no, commanded—to make our requests known unto God with thanksgiving. This does not always mean that God will give us exactly what we ask in exactly the manner in which we expect it, as we shall notice in our discussion of faith and prayer. It does mean, however, that as we recognize the constant and unlimited concern of the Father for all that affects our lives, as we quietly and in faith present our problems and ourselves to him, we come to know that all the resources of heaven are available for the solution of our problems. It is this life of prayer which leads to the "peace of God, which passes all understanding" (v. 7).

For what may we pray? What may we expect to receive from God in answer to our petition? The answer of Scripture is, "Anything" (John 14:14; cf. Matt. 21:22). Everything that concerns the child of God concerns the Father. However, there are a number of suggestions in the New Testament accounts that might guide us into the proper channels of petition.

To begin with what may be the least important petition but one that often assumes giant proportions in our lives, we may pray for "daily bread" (Matt. 6:11). We have already noticed that this petition stands for more than is expressed; it includes all that is necessary in a material way for our life on this earth—food, clothing, shelter, health, etc. There is no indication in the Scriptures that the Christian is to think that such things are secular and unworthy as objects of petition. Of course, the secularness or sacredness of daily sustenance depends on the secularness or sacredness of the life that is sustained. We are encouraged to believe that we may ask God to sustain our lives with the necessities of a material nature and that he will do so.

Let us notice, however, that this is a good illustration of the general principle of prayer that God will do nothing for us that we can do for ourselves. Prayer is not a lazy man's escape from the struggles of life. Before we can expect God to provide for us, we must seek to provide for ourselves. Paul condemns without stint the brother "who is living in idleness" and commands that the Christians imitate him and his co-workers, saying, "We did not eat any one's bread without paying, but with toil and labor we worked night and day, that we might not burden any of you." He commands that the Christian who will "not work" should not be permitted to "eat" (II Thess. 3:6-10). Not only Paul's command, but Paul's example, teaches that God's answer to our prayer for "daily bread" does not eliminate the necessity of our working and seeking to provide for ourselves, but enforces it.

We will not need to repeat this principle with reference to every other petition, but we do need to remind ourselves that it is a principle, that it applies to spiritual as well as to material blessings. The petitions we offer to God are really petitions to bless our own efforts and labors and make them effective insofar as they can be effective and to add to them when they must be supplemented. If we pray in such a spirit as this, we may be sure that God will hear and answer our requests.

What we have said opens the way for the child of God to pray concerning all the matters that relate to his everyday life. Zechariah was assured by the angel, "Your prayer is heard, and your wife Elizabeth will bear you a son" (Luke 1:13). If petition can be the means by which God can send a son, it can be the means by which God can supply all the needs of our lives. It would certainly seem true that the Christian may, and should, petition God concerning all the matters of life. A marriage should not be consummated without the consciousness of God's approval. A career should not be chosen without his guidance. Concerns of family, of health, of income, may be brought to God in petition.

More will be said in the next section about it, but we should notice that this is not a way that is open to all men regardless of their purpose in life. If we expect God to be concerned and to act creatively in the everyday affairs of our lives, we must seek his help, because we seek to serve him. The line of connection between life purpose and God's providence is traced clearly by Jesus. He says, "Seek first his kingdom and his righteousness, and all these things shall be yours as well" (Matt. 6:33). What is proposed here is a sort of human-divine partnership. God proposes that we shall invest our whole life in this partnership enterprise and he, in turn, will invest all his resources. Out of the common fund, each may call for the supply of all his needs. We make "his kingdom and his righteousness" our major concern; he undertakes to supply the needs of our lives in return. This is the way it should be in all families. What concerns one concerns all.

This is the way it can be in the "family of God." This is the privilege and responsibility that is involved in the practice of petitionary prayer.

Another class of petitions that are suggested by the teaching of the New Testament are those which have to do with our spiritual growth and maturity as children of God. We are commanded to "grow in the grace and knowledge of our Lord and Savior Jesus Christ" (II Peter 3:18). The aim of God for the Christian is expressed by Paul in the words: "For those whom he foreknew he also predestined to be conformed to the image of his Son, in order that he might be the first-born among many brethren" (Rom. 8:29). To be "conformed to the image of his Son" should be the major desire and concern of the Christian, just as it is the purpose of God. Yet this is not a task which the Christian performs by himself. The basic virtues of the Christian life, such as "love, joy, peace, patience, kindness, goodness, faithfulness, gentleness, self-control," are called the "fruit of the Spirit" by Paul (Gal. 5:22–23). The implication of this statement is that the Christian is able to grow and develop in his spiritual nature only through the ministry of the Holy Spirit. The Spirit can minister to us only as we pray. This would be true with respect to every enterprise of the soul as we seek to be like Christ; it is specifically related to the practice of prayer in two instances.

First, it is said to be true in relation to the development of a life of righteousness. We are taught to pray for the forgiveness of our sins (Matt. 6:12) and are assured that God will forgive us. This petition is not encouraged in order that we might take our sins lightly, but that our quest for the good life might meet with success. What Jesus envisioned in this prayer is made explicit in John. He says, "If we confess our sins, he is faithful and just, and will forgive our sins and cleanse us from all unrighteousness" (I John 1:9). Here the relation between our desire and God's action in granting our petition is made clear. Notice that the term is "sins," not "sin." The plural indicates that confession should take the form of particularizing our sins; it should never degenerate into a general recognition that we are sinful. Protestants are inclined to scoff at the Catholic confessional in which the communicant is commanded to give a detailed list of his sins in order to gain absolution. The fault with the Catholic confessional is not in the detailing of sins; it lies in the fact that the confession is made to men and "forgiveness" is supposedly mediated through priests. It is only as we are willing to confess our particular sins to God that forgiveness becomes a possibility. The relation between "confession" and "forgiveness" indicates that the confession is a petition; it is a petition for God to forgive us and reestablish a spiritual fellowship with us.

Though this happens, this is not all that happens when we pray. God not only forgives, he also cleanses us of all unrighteousness. In the prayer of petition, we receive what we ask, and more. God uses our prayer for forgiveness as a means of creating in us a life of righteousness. The recognition of something as sinful on our part, and the fellowship of God in its confession and forgiveness, leads to a purification of the soul. We come to see the reason for our sins; we come to see the road by which we may avoid them; we desire to lay them aside; we receive the power to do so. Could there be any other way in which this could be accomplished? I doubt it. Only as we pray can we be made progressively more and more like Christ.

Another spiritual need of the Christian life that is said to be supplied in answer to petitionary prayer is wisdom. "If any of you lacks wisdom, let him ask God, who gives to all men generously and without reproaching, and it will be given him." (James 1:5.) The thought connection between this verse and the preceding one is supplied by the purpose clause, "that you may be perfect and complete, lacking in nothing" (v. 4). James is discussing various factors in the Christian's life that are necessary to make him "perfect and complete." One factor that may be lacking is "wisdom." If a man lacks that, he should petition God for it and the promise is that God will give him wisdom. Just what "wisdom" means in this verse needs some clarification. The background of the word is probably found in the wisdom literature of late Judaism, a literature that is represented in the

Old Testament by the book of Proverbs. According to this concept of wisdom, the emphasis is upon the practical application of knowledge and experience. Wisdom is not the same thing as knowledge; it is the application of knowledge to the decisions of life. Here is an area in which most of us are lacking. Our lack can be supplied by the creative presence of God, which comes to us as a result of petitionary prayer.

What has been said about these two aspects of Christian growth would apply with equal force to every other aspect of life. As we recognize our need and turn to God with the request for his help, we will be supplied. To fail to practice petitionary prayer with respect to the needs of Christian growth would be sinful on the Christian's part. God stands ready, anxious, and eager to give us the help that we need to become like Christ. We should not fail to avail ourselves of the privilege of petition.

More will be said about the relation between prayer and service in a subsequent chapter. Here we note that many of the petitions that we are encouraged to address to God relate themselves to our service. Since every Christian is expected to be a servant of God, since our service is vitally related to God's rule and righteousness, we are encouraged to ask God for anything that is essential to the fulfillment of this service. Perhaps this is the thought that lies behind the suggestion of Jesus to his disciples that they pray that their flight from Jerusalem in the time of tribulation should not occur in the "winter or on the sabbath" (Matt. 24:20). Since such conditions of flight would mean great suffering and possible death to the servants of Christ, it would be proper for them to petition God to see that it did not come at such times. Whether this passage belongs in this category or not, there are several in the New Testament that do.

In his letter to Corinth, Paul suggested that "spiritual gifts" be made an object of petition. The Corinthians were abusing the gifts that they had by flaunting them before their less gifted brethren. They misunderstood the nature and purpose of the gifts. Because of their unchristian attitude toward the gifts of the spirit, we may be led to suppose that there is something wrong with having spiritual gifts. However, Paul never condemns the gifts; he does condemn the abuse of them. The whole tenor of his discussion (I Cor., chs. 12 to 14) indicates that he thinks the gifts are essential to fruitful Christian service. They come from God; they are to be exercised for the good of the whole body of Christ. He admonishes the Corinthians: "Earnestly desire the higher gifts" (I Cor. 12:31). If one has a gift that is useless by itself, he should pray for the supplementary gift to make it useful. "He who speaks in a tongue should pray for the power to interpret." (I Cor. 14:13.)

Another object of petition that is related to service is prayer for the opportunity to serve. This thought lies behind the message of Paul to the Roman church: "Without ceasing I mention you always in my prayers, asking that somehow by God's will I may now at last succeed in coming to you. For I long to see you, that I may impart to you some spiritual gift to strengthen you" (Rom. 1:9–11). He also assured the Thessalonians that he prayed "earnestly night and day that we may see you face to face and supply what is lacking in your faith" (I Thess. 3:10). In both instances, Paul's petition was inspired by his desire to have the opportunity to serve. These churches had problems and needs that Paul felt he could be used to meet. However, he lacked opportunity. Therefore he made the matter an object of prayer to God. Surely such a prayer is Christian and may be used by us without doubt.

When we analyze the various petitions that are urged upon us in the New Testament, we find that we should pray for those things which are needful in our everyday life in the world, such as bread, protection, children, safe journey. We should pray as well for those things which are needful in our spiritual development, such as the forgiveness of sins, the deliverance from temptation, and wisdom to make the right decisions in life. Finally, we should pray for those things which are necessary to our Christian service, such as spiritual gifts and the Holy Spirit. What a catalog of blessings awaits us if we but heed the admonition to pray!

Intercession—Synopsis

The practice of intercession rests upon the solid ground of Biblical precept and example.

The power of intercessory prayer is a mystery. It cannot be explained by its results in the lives of those who pray, nor by the effects wrought in a person's life by his knowing that others are concerned about him, nor by the power of mental telepathy. We believe that intercessory prayer makes available to God our love and concern. Thus, God uses intercessory prayer to accomplish results in the lives of men and in the course of history which he could not otherwise accomplish.

The power of intercessory prayer is almost unlimited. It has power to change the course of secular history as we pray for rulers. It has power to help bring about the salvation of the lost, the deliverance of endangered friends, and the growth of Christians in Christlikeness. By praying for others, we share in the missionary work of the world. By praying for the "sinning brother," we may help to restore him to a life of righteousness.

Intercessory prayer for the sick is a teaching of the New Testament.

VI

Forms of Prayer: Intercession

Intercession, petition to the Father in behalf of someone else, is a vital element of prayer in the New Testament. "Confess your sins to one another, and pray for one another." (James 5:16.) "Pray for those who persecute you." (Matt. 5:44.) "Pray for us." (Heb. 13:18.) "I urge that . . . intercessions . . . be made for all men." (I Tim. 2:1.) These verses are only a sampling of the passages in the New Testament that speak of the prayer of intercession as a Christian duty. The writers of the New Testament felt that prayer for others would be effective in changing the lives of men and conditions in the world.

The practice of intercession took its point of departure from the example of Jesus, both in his earthly life and in his heavenly ministry. He urged his disciples to pray for their enemies; he set the example of this type of prayer when he prayed for the forgiveness of his tormentors while he was hanging on the cross (Luke 23:34). He reminded Peter that he had prayed for him (Luke 22:32). It is probable that he had prayed for others as well. He wept over Jerusalem; no doubt he had prayed for the city and its inhabitants. He had compassion on the shepherdless multitudes; no doubt he had prayed for their conversion. He was grieved by the slowness of heart of his own disciples; no doubt he had prayed for their growth and development. Though sparse mention is made of his intercessory prayers, there can be no doubt that Jesus practiced intercession constantly. His high-priestly prayer, as we have noted, was largely composed of intercession for the Eleven and for his future disciples.

Jesus not only practiced intercession during his earthly ministry; it was the conviction of the early Christians that his intercession was a continuing reality in heaven. He had promised the disciples that he would "pray the Father, and he will give you another Counselor, to be with you for ever" (John 14:16). Pentecost, with all its wondrous events, came, we may believe, quite as much as a result of the prayer of Jesus as of the prayers of the disciples (cf. Acts 1:14). John encouraged his readers to live without sin but reminded them, "If any one does sin, we have an advocate with the Father, Jesus Christ the righteous" (I John 2:1). To John, the intercessory ministry of Jesus was an encouragement both to strive for perfection and to seek forgiveness when our striving fails. Using the analogy of the priesthood, the writer of Hebrews insists that the reason Jesus can save those "for all time . . . who draw near to God through him" is that "he always lives to make intercession for them" (Heb. 7:25).

We may never be able to understand all that the heavenly ministry of Jesus means. Perhaps it is a figurative way of expressing his continued concern for and his involvement in the life of his people. We cannot escape the conclusion that early Christians believed that Jesus had practiced intercession and continued to do so. In this matter, as in all others, he set an example that we "should follow in his steps" (I Peter 2:21).

Paul also practiced intercession. Most of his letters open with a benediction on his readers and close with one or more benedictions. Though these expressions of concern may be explained by the epistolary style of that day, we may be certain, I think, that they constituted genuine intercessory prayers on the part of Paul. His letters are filled with assertions of his concern and prayer for his readers. He assured the Colossians that he had not ceased to pray for them since the day he had heard of their faith (Col. 1:9). This statement indicates some kind of list that Paul may have kept to remind him of the constant need of the churches for his prayers. He asserted that he "constantly" mentioned the Thessalonians in his prayers (I Thess. 1:2). He reminded Timothy of his thankfulness for him and assured him that he "constantly" remembered Timothy when he prayed (II Tim.

1:3). In this matter as in most matters related to the Christian life, Paul stands head and shoulders above all other Christians in his practice of following the example of the Master.

Paul's belief in the power of intercessory prayer is seen in his repeated appeals to his readers to pray for him. He believed that the experience of God's power in his own ministry rested, to some degree, on the faithfulness of the churches in praying for him. He appealed to the Romans to strive together with him in their prayers to God on his behalf (Rom. 15:30–32). He reminded the Corinthians that they also must help him "by prayer" so that his ministry would lead many to give thanks to God (II Cor. 1:11). He asked the Ephesians to pray for him that his mouth might be opened to boldly "proclaim the mystery of the gospel" (Eph. 6:19). He pleaded with the Colossians to pray that God might open to him a door for the word (Col. 4:3–4). He urged the Thessalonians to pray for him (I Thess. 5:25). He expressed his belief that the prayer of the church at Philippi (Phil. 1:19) and of his friend, Philemon (Philemon 22), would lead to his release from prison. Such appeals on the part of Paul reveal that he thought of the gospel enterprise as a missionary fellowship of all Christians, those on the battlefront and those in the churches.

Not only Paul, but other Christians as well, practiced the ministry of intercession. The church at Colossae was reminded that Epaphras, one of their own number, though absent from them, continued to strive earnestly for them in his prayers on their behalf (Col. 4:12). This emphasis on intercessory prayer, though it is much stronger in the New Testament than in the Old, is in harmony with the practice of Old Testament leaders. Moses repeatedly interceded with God in behalf of the nation during the wilderness wanderings. Samuel told the people of Israel that though they had rejected the Kingship of God in favor of an earthly king, he would continue to pray for them. He said, "Moreover as for me, far be it from me that I should sin against the Lord by ceasing to pray for you." (I Sam. 12:23.) The practice of intercession rests upon the solid foundation of Biblical command and examples.

How can the prayer of one man change the life of another?

The problem of prayer becomes most acute when we speak of intercession. It seems to be the teaching of the New Testament that intercessory prayer enables God to do something in the life of the one who was prayed for *which he could not otherwise do*. This seems preposterous to the unbeliever and shakes the confidence of many Christians. We who are Christians claim to believe the Bible, but often our belief is more intellectual than dynamic. We say we believe, but our belief does not lead us to practice. Belief that is not strong enough to change our practice is very weak indeed. I suppose that one area of Christian life where most Christians utterly fail is the area of the practice of intercessory prayer. Our belief in its efficacy seems to fall short of dynamic belief.

The explanation of the power of intercessory prayer is not found in its effect on the one who prays. It has been suggested that one is led to enlarge his own concern and deepen his own love for others by praying for them. This may be true, but it is not the New Testament explanation of the power of intercessory prayer. The one who prays may be led to discover ways in which he can act for others to help them when he prays. This also is true. Certainly one who makes a habit of praying for others is made more like Jesus; his horizon of life is enlarged; his concern for others is deepened; his life is pulled out of the morass of selfishness into which most of us tend to sink. But all of this falls short of the New Testament conception of the power of intercessory prayer. For instance, Paul believed that the prayers of the Philippian church and of his friend in the ministry, Philemon, would have power to effect his release from the Roman imprisonment. The writer of The Acts believed that the prayer of the church at Jerusalem led to the deliverance of Peter from jail (Acts 12:5–11). There is no way in which these experiences can be explained by referring the power of prayer to the one who prays. Neither the Philippians nor the church at Jerusalem could be used to effect the release. Their concern may have helped their Christian growth, but it would not have helped Paul unless there is more to intercessory prayer than this. No, it seems that the New Testament writers felt that God was enabled to act with power through the prayers of one man for another.

Others have assumed that the power of intercessory prayer lies in the awareness of it by the persons for whom one prays. The life of the person for whom we pray is changed because he knows we are concerned for him. This is only a partial explanation, though it is true. The unsaved man is often moved to seek salvation because he is aware of the prayers of others for him. The Christian servant is often encouraged by the love and concern of others for him. One denomination of Christians makes a practice of listing the names of home and foreign missionaries for the prayers of the people on the date of each missionary's birth. Many of the missionaries have testified that they have felt a fresh inspiration and endowment from the Holy Spirit as a result. Part of that result may be explained by the fact that they know that others will pray for them on this day. Certainly, the New Testament would encourage us to let others in on the secret of our prayer and concern for them. Paul made no secret of his prayers for his readers and friends; he not only told them that he did pray for them; he often detailed the particular petitions that he offered up to God in their behalf. No doubt he felt that their knowledge of his prayers would make it possible for God to answer them more readily.

However, this explanation does not do justice to all that is involved in the Christian belief with regard to intercessory prayer. For instance, Christians are urged to pray "for kings and all who are in high positions" (I Tim. 2:2). In the first century, such men would be wholly unaware of the prayers of the Christians for them. They would have been amused if they had known. Yet Paul seemed to feel that such prayers had power to change the political climate of his day. They would enable God to move in the lives of the earthly authorities so that Christians might "lead a quiet and peaceable life." Thus the power of intercessory prayer goes beyond the effect that is wrought in a man's heart by his knowledge that others are concerned about him.

Nor can mental telepathy explain the power of intercessory

prayer. It may be, as some have insisted, that there is more to mental telepathy than most men are willing to admit. Even if we assume that it is possible for one man to project his own will into the life of another by this method, it would not explain what happens when one man prays for another. Aside from the fact that conclusions about the power of mental telepathy are still highly speculative, the purpose of such efforts is not at all the same as the purpose of intercessory prayer. Mental telepathy seeks to project the will of one man into the life of another; intercessory prayer seeks to open the way for *God's will* to be done in the life of another. Most Christians would consider the projection of their will into the life of someone else a violation of human rights. Even if it were possible, they would avoid its use. The intercessor seeks to enable God to act redemptively and creatively in the lives of men and in the course of history. He prays because he believes that his prayer will open the way for God to act in ways in which he could not otherwise act.

It must be admitted that there is no rational explanation of this belief. It is impossible even to prove that intercessory prayer accomplishes anything. There are examples, many, if all of them were known, in which someone prayed for something to happen to others, and it did happen. But it is impossible to establish scientifically a cause-effect relationship between the prayer and the occurrence. Too many uncontrolled and uncontrollable factors enter into human life and history. It is even impossible to be dogmatic about the New Testament examples of intercessory prayer. True, Christ promised to pray for the giving of the Holy Spirit to his church, and the Holy Spirit came. True, the church at Jerusalem did pray for the release of Peter from prison, and an angel of God brought him forth (Acts 12:11). But there is no way of *proving* that these things happened *solely* and *only* because of intercessory prayer. Perhaps God would have sent the Holy Spirit and delivered Peter from prison even if prayer had not been made for these things. The Christian believes that the prayers were the effective cause of God's actions, but he cannot prove this even to himself. No, the only basis for intercessory prayer must be faith, faith in a creative and redemptive Father who has invited us to share in his burden of love and concern for the world. Faith must be its own authentication.

How, then, can the power of intercessory prayer be explained? Need we say that the purpose of intercessory prayer is not to persuade God to do something that he is reluctant to do? Some pray as if this were true. God does not need to be persuaded to do what he should; he cannot be persuaded to do what he should not. The Christian feels that his burden of prayer for others is created by God; God initiates intercessory prayer just as he does petitionary prayer. How, then, can our prayer help? It must be thought of as enabling God to do what he wishes to do in history and the lives of others. This is the mystery of intercession. Our praying makes our concern available to God in solving the problems of others and of the world. This is a mystery; it is not magic. Our concern, conscious and expressed in prayer, becomes a part of the armory of God in achieving his design in the world. This is why Samuel thought it would be a "sin against the Lord" for him to cease his praying for Israel (I Sam. 12:23). To fail to pray for others is to withhold from God something that he desires and needs from us. Failure to practice intercessory prayer is the same kind of sin as failure to witness to Christ.

What can God accomplish through intercessory prayer? The answer is suggested by New Testament passages on the subject —suggested but not exhausted. I think it is fair to assume that New Testament writers felt that their prayers of intercession included those things which God could accomplish through them. Therefore the passages on intercessory prayer may suggest the lines of our intercession. It would not, however, be true to assume that nothing else could be the object of intercession. Conditions have changed. The details of our prayers will undoubtedly be different from those of Paul. The principles will be the same.

The power of intercessory prayer is almost unlimited, if the New Testament is to be believed. S. D. Gordon argues that prayer is the greatest outlet of power that is available to the Christian. He lists five outlets of power: the life we live, the words we speak to others, the service we perform, the money we give, and the prayers we pray. Of all these, he conceives of prayer as the greatest because it enables the Christian to have a world ministry.[39] His conclusions are in line with New Testament teachings. The Christian, through the practice of intercessory prayer, may stand by the side of a governor and help him rule the world wisely and well; he may stand by the side of an unsaved friend and help him decide for Christ; he may stand by the side of an endangered one and help him to safety; he may stand in the sickroom and help the sick to regain health; he may stand by the side of a missionary and help him to witness as he should; he may stand by the side of his Christian brethren and help them to become like Christ; he may have a ministry in many churches as he prays for the development and power of those churches.

The material for study is not great, but a word might be said about intercessory prayer for "kings and all who are in high positions," that the people may lead a "quiet and peaceable life, godly and respectful in every way" (I Tim. 2:2). This is the only passage in the New Testament that enjoins prayer for political rulers, though the practice of the Jewish nation in offering sacrifices for the rulers, and the admonition of Paul (Rom. 13:1) and Peter (I Peter 2:13) that we be subject to human powers and consider them as servants of God would certainly imply that this was a duty universally felt among the early Christians. Paul thought of intercessory prayer as a means by which we might bring, or help to bring, the will of God to pass in the secular affairs of the world.

When we consider the nature of the government, spiritually speaking, in the first century, we may be put to shame because we do not take more seriously our responsibility to pray for our own leaders. If intercessory prayer could be thought to affect the rule of Nero, surely it can have power in the lives of men who, either consciously or unconsciously, are influenced by Christian principles of action. One of the beautiful heritages of American history is the speech of Benjamin Franklin when he rose to move that the Constitutional Convention be opened with prayer each morning. He reminded the delegates of the fact that daily prayers for divine protection had been offered in that very room during the conflict with Britain. He pointed out that it was only through the superintending providence of God that the war had been won and that the opportunity to meet and draw up a constitution for the new nation had come.

He reproached the delegates for seeming to forget their divine Friend and supposing that they no longer needed his aid. "I have lived, Sir, a long time and the longer I live the more convincing proofs I see of the truth; that God governs in the affairs of men. And if a sparrow cannot fall to the ground without his notice, is it probable that an empire can rise without his aid? ... I ... believe that without his concurring aid we shall succeed in this political building no better than the builders of Babel."[40]

If a professed deist could make such a stirring challenge to prayer for the new nation, how much more should those of us who claim to be Christian pray for our nation and the nations of the world today. It may well be that the "days of prayer" by the nation and the constant intercession of Christian patriots may have more to do with establishing a lasting peace in our world than all the efforts of the United Nations.

We need to notice, with reference to this object of prayer, that the final purpose of peace is not peace but the opportunity to evangelize the world and glorify God. This is the place where politicians and Christians can never see eye to eye unless they be one and the same. The statesman wants peace because of its benefits for the world. The Christian seeks peace so that the gospel may have swift passage into the hearts of men.

Next, let us notice that intercessory prayer is thought to have efficacy in the salvation of the lost. Though not many instances of prayer for the lost are recorded in the New Testament, there are sufficient indications of it to justify belief in its efficacy at this point. To this category belong those passages which command prayer for our enemies. In every case, where the objective of such prayer is mentioned, it is for the forgiveness and salvation of the enemy—for his good. No instances of imprecation exist in the New Testament. One passage seems to pronounce a curse, but the appearance of imprecation is based on a mistranslation in the King James Version: "Alexander the coppersmith did me much evil: the Lord reward him according to his works." (II Tim. 4:14, KJV). The Greek word behind "the Lord reward him" is in the future tense and is correctly rendered in the Revised Standard Version as, "The Lord will requite him for his deeds." Both Jesus (Luke 23:34) and Stephen (Acts 7:60) prayed for the forgiveness of those who put them to death. Paul prayed for those who had forsaken him: "At my first defense no one took my part; all deserted me. May it not be charged against them!" (II Tim. 4:16). To this subject may also be related the statement of Paul that he would be willing to be accursed for the sake of Israel if only they could be saved (Rom. 9:3), and his further statement, "Brethren, my heart's desire and prayer to God for them is that they may be saved" (Rom. 10:1). Finally, we may mention the expressed wish of Paul to Agrippa. In response to Agrippa's sneering remark that Paul was trying to convert him, Paul said, "I would to God that not only you but also all who hear me this day might become such as I am—except for these chains" (Acts 26:29). The indications are sufficient in these passages to teach that the New Testament writers thought of intercessory prayer as a means by which they might cooperate with God in the salvation of lost men.

Christians may also help to protect their friends from physical danger and help to deliver them from prison through the practice of intercessory prayer. Peter's release from prison, on one occasion at least, is directly connected with intercessory prayer by the church (Acts 12:5–11). Paul believed that his release from prison would be effected and that the prayers of the church at Philippi would be causes that would contribute to it (Phil. 1:19) and of his friend, Philemon (Philemon 22). He urged the Roman church to pray for his deliverance from the "unbelievers in Judea" (Rom. 15:31). This would seem to indicate that the Christian may participate in the physical safety and deliverance of his friends through the practice of intercessory prayer.

Intercessory prayer, as we have noted, may be the instrument of forming a world brotherhood for the conversion of the lost. Many times, the modern Christian thinks of missionaries as representatives of the churches who carry the gospel of Christ to foreign lands. Our main concern is to support them with our money, to free their hands from secular labor, that they might, with the help of God, convert the heathen. This does not follow the pattern of the New Testament. Paul thought of the gospel enterprise as a joint undertaking of all Christians. Though some would go abroad and others would stay at home, all were deeply involved in the work of witnessing.

According to Paul, the primary responsibility of those who stayed at home was intercessory prayer. Financial support was often received and appreciated, but spiritual support through prayer was constantly admonished. We have cited a number of passages above in which Paul appealed to his readers to pray for him. One passage is worthy of special notice because it emphasizes the idea of teamwork in the gospel enterprise. "I appeal to you, brethren, by our Lord Jesus Christ and by the love of the Spirit, to strive together with me in your prayers to God on my behalf." (Rom. 15:30.) Though the immediate concern of Paul in this prayer is the risk that he takes in going to Jerusalem, the ultimate concern is that he shall be able to carry on his work of evangelization in Rome and Spain. The phrase "Strive together with me in your prayers to God on my behalf" presents a graphic picture of the missionary and the church standing side by side on the battlefront, confronting and overcoming the enemy, he by his preaching, they by their prayers for him. He admonished the Corinthians: "You also must help us by prayer" (II Cor. 1:11).

Next, we notice the part that intercessory prayer plays in the Christian ministry, a part that was considerable in the New Testament, even though it may be much neglected today. Paul commends Epaphras to the Colossian church and reminds the Colossians that he was "always laboring fervently" for them in prayers, that they might "stand perfect and complete in all the will of God" (Col. 4:12, KJV). The ministry of prayer to which the Jerusalem apostles wished to give themselves no doubt included intercessory prayer, though this is not specifically mentioned (Acts 6:4). The major material for study here is found in the recorded prayers of Paul for his churches.[41] He prayed for the Roman church, that God might grant the Christians there to live in "harmony with one another, in accord with Christ Jesus," that together they might "with one voice glorify the God and Father" of their Lord Jesus Christ (Rom. 15:5–6). For the Ephesians, he prayed that they might have the "spirit of wisdom and of revelation" in the knowledge of God and thus be able to understand the hope to which God has called them, the riches of God's inheritance, and the power of God operating in their lives (Eph. 1:16–19). Again, he prayed that they might "be strengthened with might through his Spirit in the inner man" and thus come to experience the indwelling presence of Christ and to understand the greatness of his love (Eph. 3:14–19). His prayer for the Colossians and those who had not seen his face in the flesh was that their hearts might be encouraged as they were "knit together in love, to have all the riches of assured understanding" (Col. 2:1–2). For the Philippians, he prayed for a continuing increase in their love, so that they might approve "what is excellent," and might be "pure and blameless for the day of Christ, filled with the fruits of righteousness which come through Jesus Christ, to the glory and praise of God" (Phil. 1:9–11). For the Thessalonians, he prayed, "May the Lord make you increase and abound in love to one another and to all men, as we do to you, so that he may establish your hearts unblamable in holiness before our God and Father, at the coming of our Lord Jesus with all his saints" (I Thess. 3:12–13). Again, he prayed that "God may make you worthy of his call, and may fulfil every good resolve and work of faith by his power" (II Thess. 1:11). As we read these prayers of Paul's, we are impressed with the wide range of what he asks for his churches through intercessory prayer:—harmony, love, power, strength, growth, etc. It would seem certain that he considered it possible through his prayers to continue to minister to the churches even when absent from them.

Mention should also be made of the range of blessings that New Testament writers pronounced upon their readers in the opening and closing benedictions of the epistles. They include such things as comfort, establishment of heart, faith, love, mercy, grace, joy, peace, and hope.[42] There is a remarkable similarity between these benedictions and those things which are "fruit of the Spirit" listed by Paul as the primary virtues of the Christian life (cf. Gal. 5:22–23).

The final aspect of spiritual service through intercessory prayer is found in the admonition that Christians should pray for their Christian brothers who sin. John says, "If any one sees his brother sinning a sin which is not, in his opinion, unto death, he shall ask, and he will give him life" (I John 5:16, my translation). There are many problems of interpretation connected with this passage, but the one clear, shining certainty is that the Christian should pray (the future is imperative in force here) for any of his brothers whom he sees committing a sin. It is not our business, in such a case, to tell everybody about the sin of our brother; it is, rather, our business as Christians to make our prayer and our life available to God in reclaiming the brother for a life of righteousness. The qualifying phrase "not unto death" (the Revised Standard Version translation, "mortal sin," is, to say the least, misleading here) probably is intended to teach that such prayer is not to be a superficial matter, but a matter of deep concern and faith. The Greek negative in this case is the subjective negative and points to the opinion of the Christian brother who is to pray, not to the real nature of the sin. The verse could probably with correctness be paraphrased somewhat in this manner: "It is your duty to use prayer as a vehicle of God's redemptive work in behalf of your brother. If, therefore, you see your brother commit a sin and if you believe his sin is not one that places him beyond reclaiming, you are obligated to pray for him and God will give him life." Of course, if, in the opinion of the one praying, the sin places the brother "beyond redemption," he could not in good conscience pray for the forgiveness of the sinning one. He could not pray with faith; therefore he should not pray at all. John adds, "There is a sin unto death; I do not say that one should pray in behalf of that" (v. 16b, my translation).

The New Testament does not encourage us to believe that our prayer to God for the forgiveness of others will actually accomplish that forgiveness apart from their own confession of sin and plea for forgiveness. What we are to think is that our concern, when shared with God, will in some way make it possible for God to bring our brother to see the error of his way, repent, and receive forgiveness from a gracious Father.

Another object of intercessory prayer is bodily healing. We must, I think, make a careful distinction between the miraculous power to heal and healing in answer to intercessory prayer. Jesus and his apostles, and perhaps a number of other persons, exercised the "gifts of healing" (I Cor. 12:9). Even so, the healing often was accompanied by an act of prayer. Peter is said to have prayed before he commanded the good Tabitha (Dorcas) to arise from the dead (Acts 9:40). It is recorded that Paul visited the father of Publius "and prayed, and putting his hands on him healed him" (Acts 28:8). In both of these cases the healing seems to have taken place as a result of the exercise of miraculous powers; the praying was secondary. This kind of power, according to my opinion, was limited to the apostolic age. It was designed to authenticate the messengers of God when there was no standard of measurement such as the New Testament.

Of a different nature is the promise of healing through intercessory prayer. "Is any among you sick? Let him call for the elders of the church, and let them pray over him, anointing him with oil in the name of the Lord; and the prayer of faith will save the sick man, and the Lord will raise him up; and if he has committed sins, he will be forgiven." (James 5:14–15.) This is a unique passage in the New Testament; no other passage speaks of healing in answer to prayer. However, it seems to reflect a widespread belief among early Christians that intercessory prayer was effective in healing the sick. We find references to the practice of prayer for the sick in the Epistles of Clement, Ignatius, and Polycarp.[43]

Several elements in the passage in James are worthy of notice: the sick man who may also stand in need of forgiveness of sin, the elders of the church who are called in, the anointing with oil, the prayer of faith, and the promise of recovery. There may be a suggestion that the sickness, at least in part, was due to sin, but this is uncertain. The passage would not limit the efficacy of intercessory prayer for the sick to those cases caused by sin. We may suppose that the "elders of the congregation" were called because they represented the most devout men among the Christians. We are not to suppose that this would limit the prayer of healing to the clergy; any man of faith may offer it quite as effectively.

The use of oil for "anointing" the sick man may be interpreted either as a ritual or as a medical anointing. "Oil was believed to have the effect of curing bodily sickness."[44] This is perhaps the real reason for its use in this case. If so, it would suggest that the prayer for healing should be accompanied by the employment of all medical resources. Prayer should not be a substitute for medicine; the two resources for healing should be used at the same time. The man of medicine and the man of faith should constitute a healing team. The complementary nature of medicine and faith is being increasingly recognized today; the idea seems to have a firm foundation in this passage.

The prayer that heals is said to be the "prayer of faith." The faith of the sick man is not mentioned, but is probably implied in his appeal to the elders to pray for him. It is the faith of the intercessors that is emphasized in this passage. This would mean that the elders, or others who pray for the sick, yield their concern and faith into the hands of God to be used by him in his gracious work of healing.

The promise, "The Lord will raise him up," is not, I think, to be taken as absolute. There is no justification in the New Testament that the "prayer of faith" will always result in healing. If this were true, all who die would die because their faith failed. This is an unthinkable conclusion. Rather, when healing does occur, it is to be recognized as the work of the Lord, not as the result of some natural power.

Our modern preoccupation with the power of science has tended to blind us to the healing power of intercessory prayer. Also, more conservative Christians are repelled by the excesses of fanaticism in some modern movements of healing. We must remember that all healing is from God. This is true even when it takes place wholly through the practice of medicine. Medical science has never learned to heal anybody. It has only learned, and this imperfectly, to use the means that God has created to arrest the progress of disease and give nature a chance to heal the disease. To the man of faith, "nature" is just a name to describe the ordinary workings of God's providential presence in the world. The healing is of God. If this be so, why should it be thought strange that intercessory prayer, if it has power anywhere, would have power here as well?

Commitment—Synopsis

Effective prayer is that prayer which accomplishes the will of God in the life of the worshiper and in the world.

Only the Christian can pray effectively. The sinner has no promise for answered prayer except the prayer for salvation.

Before the Christian can pray effectively he must be serious in his quest for the Christlike life.

Before the Christian can pray effectively he must establish and maintain right relationships with his fellowman.

Before the Christian can pray effectively he must become involved in the service of Christ. Prayer "in Jesus' name" has unlimited power, but only those who live "in Jesus' name," i.e., as his representatives on earth, can pray in his name.

This chapter is not so much a discussion of conditions of effective prayer as it is a discussion of the kind of person who can pray effectively.

VII

Effective Prayer: Commitment

When we speak of effective prayer, we are not talking about the "batting average" of the worshiper. There are those who would seem to judge the effectiveness of their prayer life by the number of "cases" that they win at the throne of God in relation to the number they lose. On the other hand, we are not talking about some kind of good feeling that arises in the heart of the one who prays. There are those who would seem to judge the effectiveness of their prayer life by the subjective feeling that one receives when he establishes communion with God.

Both of these factors enter into our judgment as to the effectiveness of our prayer life. It would seem to be true that "there must be definite, practical results, if prayer is vital."[45] Surely, if one can never point to a definite, measurable result of his prayer life, he would have reason to wonder whether he prays in vain. But the answer to prayer is more than receiving; it is communion as well. As we take our problems and difficulties to God in prayer, it may well be that God will refuse our request for a specific answer and will, instead, impress upon our hearts a course of action that will bring solution. In such a case, we would have to say that the prayer had been effective. Nothing measurable or definite has happened to which we can point as the "answer" to prayer, but prayer has been effective. The true measure of the effectiveness of prayer must lie in the direction of how vitally our prayer life relates itself to the accomplishment of the will of God in us and in the world. The purpose of prayer is to accomplish not the will of man but the will of God. Perhaps this means three things in relation to prayer.[46] (1) It means that the one who prays is brought into harmony with the will of God. Prayer is effective to the extent to which it changes the heart and desire of the one who prays so that he conforms to God's desire for his life. We have not truly been successful in prayer until our will becomes the same as his will. (2) It means that the one who prays receives fresh accessions of divine power, so that he may actually do the will of God. The experience of prayer should result in power—spiritual power. If it does not do this for the worshiper, prayer is ineffective and meaningless. (3) It means that as a result of prayer, the will of God is accomplished in the lives of other men and in the world. The power of prayer is not limited, if we are to believe the New Testament, to its effects in the life of the individual. Prayer may reach out and work changes in any relationship or situation in the world. Unless prayer does this, it could hardly be called effective prayer.

But how may one judge the effectiveness of his prayer life? This is a difficult question. Perhaps it is an unnecessary question. What we are concerned about is not so much a way by which we may point to the results of our own prayers but a way by which we can learn to pray more effectively. Most of us would hesitate to say, "I prayed and this happened. If I had not prayed, it would not have happened. My prayer brought it to pass." If we could say this consistently, it would probably foster in our hearts a spirit of self-righteousness and kill any real prayer.

In this matter, as in so many others in our religion, we must seek the guidance of the New Testament and seek to pray in the manner and spirit that is taught there. We then must believe that God will answer our prayer because he has promised to do so. This is the first step on the road to assurance in prayer. As we mature, our communion with God may develop to the point that we may be conscious, even while praying, that God has answered our prayer and the result desired will take place.

What are the principles of prayer that we must learn in order to have assurance that our prayer is effective? These will be discussed in this and the following two chapters. I have attempted to gather up the material of the New Testament that would ordinarily be discussed under the heading of "conditions" of effective prayer and "hindrances" to effective prayer under three headings: commitment, faith, and perseverance.

The first of these, the subject of this chapter, is not really a discussion of the manner and method of praying but of the manner and kind of person who can pray effectively. One might know all about the manner and method of making out and signing a proper check, but unless he has a bank account, his check, no matter how correctly written, will be of no value. Often men speak as if there were some kind of magic formula or way of prayer that any man might use with power regardless of his own personal relationship to God and his own personal character. This popular conception of prayer finds its contradiction in the New Testament.

Only the committed can pray effectively; only those who are involved with all their being in the redemptive program of God can pray with power. This means that only a Christian can pray effectively. But it means more; it means that only the practicing Christian can pray effectively. The practicing Christian is that Christian who is serious in his quest for the righteous life, who seeks to live in loving fellowship with his fellowmen, and who is involved in Kingdom service.

On one occasion Jesus healed a man who had been born blind. When the Pharisees questioned the man and learned that Jesus had made clay and anointed the man's eyes on the Sabbath, they said, "Give God the praise; we know that this man is a sinner" (John 9:24). The healed man could not accept the judgment of the Pharisees; his eyes were open. He knew that the power of God had operated in his life. Quoting a proverbial saying of the Jews, he said, "We know that God does not listen to sinners, but if any one is a worshiper of God and does his will, God listens to him. Never since the world began has it been heard that any one opened the eyes of a man born blind. If this man were not from God, he could do nothing" (vs. 31–33).

This saying was reported by John because he felt that it summarized the teachings of God about the kind of man who could pray effectively. Notice the statements: "We know that God does not listen to sinners," and "If this man were not from God, he could do nothing." The work of Jesus, manifestly a demonstration of the power of God, was used by the man born blind to prove that Jesus was from God, that he was a worshiper of God who made a practice of doing God's will. It may be used by us to learn that we must be this kind of man before we can hope to have an effective prayer life.

This means, first of all, that a man must be a Christian before he can pray effectively. There is no record in the New Testament of effective prayer on the part of ungodly and sinful men. Even if we included as prayers the appeals of men to Jesus, we would find that faith is said to have accompanied appeal in almost every instance. It is always the thought of the New Testament that prayer is for the Christian and for him alone.

Someone might object to this. We have all heard testimonies given by men that they had prayed and God had helped them even before they were saved. Perhaps the most usual of these is after the pattern of one soldier in time of peril. He said: "I prayed to God for help; there was nowhere else to turn. He answered and saved me from my danger." We need not deny the truth of this testimony. Of course it may be true that God answered the prayers of a godly mother or concerned friends when he saved the soldier. There is no way of proving that the prayer of the soldier was the effective cause of God's protection. However, it might have been. The goodness of God, even to godless man, is beyond the imagination of man. We have the word of Jesus that God sends the rain and the sunshine on the unjust as well as the just. Paul reminds us that the goodness of God, visited on ungodly men, is meant to lead them to repentance (Rom. 2:4).

What I am saying is that there is no teaching of the New Testament that would encourage the sinner to think that he can pray with effectiveness. No example is given of God answering the prayer of such men as Judas, Pilate, or Caiaphas. No promise is given that God will answer the prayer of the unsaved. Modern men who with superficial religiosity pronounce the blessings of God on their friends while their lives deny any real surrender to God's rule are not really religious. One man is reported to have said when he won an important boxing contest, "Somebody up there likes me." Such talk borders on blasphemy. The throne of grace is open only to the children of God; the invitation to pray is addressed only to the believer. I would not try to limit God; I would not say that he never answers the prayer of the unsaved. I would assert that a man must surrender before he can have any assurance that his prayers will be answered.

One exception, which is not really an exception, is to be noted. The sinner may pray for salvation; the sinner *is commanded* to pray for salvation. The sinner is promised that he will be saved if he prays for salvation. "Every one who calls upon the name of the Lord will be saved." (Rom. 10:13; cf. Acts 2:21; Joel 2:32.) New Testament examples of men who prayed for salvation and received it are not lacking. The dying thief cried, "Jesus, remember me when you come in your kingly power" (Luke 23:42). As one preacher put it, "Jesus stopped dying long enough to save the thief." Luke tells us that Jesus responded, "Truly, I say to you, today you will be with me in Paradise." In my opinion this is the only appeal addressed to Jesus that deserves to be considered a prayer in the true sense of the word. The case of Cornelius applies here as well. The angel said to him, "Cornelius . . . , your prayers and your alms have ascended as a memorial before God" (Acts 10:3–4). Some might think that this is an exception to our general principle stated above. However, the context shows that the particular prayer that was heard and answered was the prayer for salvation. Paul's prayer on the Damascus road might be of this nature. It is impossible to establish a chronology and decide whether Paul was saved before he prayed or after. His conversation with the risen Lord was part and parcel of his salvation experience. It contains two prayers, both of which were answered. They were, "Who are you, Lord?" and "What shall I do, Lord?" (Acts 22:8, 10). The result of the whole experience is that the persecuting Pharisee became the surrendered Christian. So far as the evidence goes, the only prayer that the unsaved man may expect to be answered is the prayer for salvation.

Only the Christian can pray effectively, but not every Christian has the assurance and promise of power in prayer. The New Testament teaches that the Christian who hopes to pray with power must be a practicing Christian. He must deserve to be called by the name "Christian." We are all aware that this name is used only twice in the New Testament. One passage says, "In Antioch the disciples were for the first time called Christians" (Acts 11:26). The Greek verb for "called" (*chrēmatisai*) literally means "to transact business under a particular name" and thus to be known by that name.[47] "Christian" was probably a nickname applied in ridicule by the heathen of Antioch. Since the disciples were always talking about Christ, since they made Christ their business, they earned for themselves the name "Christian." Modern Christianity has very largely lost the implication of its name and perhaps will never recover it. However, in the practice of prayer, what the name stands for must become reality. When we say that only the Christian can pray effectively, we should include in the name all that it can mean. In relation to prayer, moreover, the New Testament details three aspects of the Christian life that must be a reality before effective prayer can become a possibility.

One of these aspects is that a man must be sincere in his quest for the Christlike life. Salvation is a gift, but it is a challenge and an invitation to a way of life. It lays the foundation for a godly life; we must build the superstructure. Paul characterized his aim in life by saying, "I am continually pressing on in pursuit of the ideal life for which Christ laid hold of me at the time of my conversion" and added, "Those of us who are grown men in the Christian religion, let us share this quest for Christian perfection" (Phil. 3:12, 15, my paraphrase). It was this sincerity of purpose in the quest for the "promised life" that qualified Paul to be a man of prayer. A similar sincerity of purpose must be ours before we can be qualified to practice at the bar of divine grace. This should not be surprising. It should be expected that only those who share the concern of God and seek the same ends as God seeks can live in a prayer partnership with God.

James states this principle both positively and negatively. "The prayer of a righteous man has great power in its effects" (James 5:16), or as it is translated in a more familiar version, "The effectual fervent prayer of a righteous man availeth much." This is the positive statement of the fact that the righteous man can pray with power. "You ask and do not receive, because you ask wrongly, to spend it on your passions" (James 4:3) is the reverse side of the same coin. The unrighteous man, the selfish Christian, cannot pray with power. Peter seeks to challenge his readers to live a righteous life. He does this by pointing to the holy character of God (I Peter 1:16–17) and quotes the psalmist, who says: "The eyes of the Lord are upon the righteous, and his ears are open to their prayer. But the face of the Lord is against them that do evil" (I Peter 3:12; cf. Ps. 34:15–16). John adds his testimony to this truth by saying, "We receive from him whatever we ask, because we keep his commandments and do what pleases him" (I John 3:22).

How stringent is this requirement? To what degree must man attain righteousness before he can pray effectively? You will notice that I have avoided saying that one must *be* righteous; I have said that one must *be serious in his quest for* righteousness. I think this represents the teaching of the New Testament at this point. Elijah is pointed to as an example of a "righteous man" who accomplished much through prayer, but he is said to have been "a man of like nature with ourselves" (James 5:17). Plainly implied in this expression is the idea that the righteousness required for effective prayer is not absolute righteousness. This could have been found only in Jesus. Yet many other men prayed with power in spite of their imperfections. Moses prayed and he was answered in spite of his impatience with God; David prayed and he was answered in spite of his serious sins; Elijah prayed and he was answered in spite of his loss of courage. Peter prayed with power, and his imperfections are well known. Paul prayed with power, though he considered himself to be far short of the ideal life. What is required is seriousness of purpose. Men cannot deliberately live outside the will and desire of God and expect God to answer their prayers consistently.

This does not mean that God will never answer the prayer of an unrighteous Christian. However, here, as in the case of the sinner, one prayer must precede all others. It is the prayer for forgiveness. We cannot expect God to be a kindly "grandfather" who comes to the rescue of his rebellious grandchildren. He is Father. As Father, his action must always be controlled by consideration of principles of righteousness.

One concern of the Christian life that is stressed in the New Testament as essential to power in prayer is our relationship with our fellowmen. This is, of course, only one phase of living righteously, but since this phase receives special emphasis in the New Testament, we must give it special notice. Perhaps the reason for the special stress on the necessity of right relationships between men as a precondition of effective prayer is to be found in the fact that "love" is the basic Christian virtue. Loving our neighbors as ourselves was listed by Jesus as the second commandment, like unto the requirement that we love God with our whole being (Mark 12:31). Love for one another is the unmistakable mark of discipleship (John 13:35). "Owe no one anything, except to love one another; for he who loves his neighbor has fulfilled the law." (Rom. 13:8.) Love is the royal law (James 2:8), the quality that "binds everything together in perfect harmony" (Col. 3:14), the first "fruit of the Spirit" (Gal. 5:22), and the greatest of all Christian virtues (I Cor. 13:13). Proper relationship with fellowmen, especially with fellow believers, must always remain one of the chief aims of the Christian.

Jesus commanded that one who came to the altar with an offering for God and remembered that his brother had something against him should leave his offering and "first be recon-

ciled" to his brother, and then come and offer his gift (Matt.
5:24). The implication of this command is that the gift will be
unacceptable so long as a person's relationship with his brother is
not what it should be. Though the teaching is given against the
background of Jewish temple worship, the same principle would
undoubtedly apply to prayer. This is made certain by Jesus'
stress on forgiveness as a necessity if we expect to receive forgiveness from the Father (Matt. 6:14–15). Love is tested most sorely
when we feel that we have been wronged; our natural inclination
is to seek retaliation. Our Christian duty is to forgive. But this is
not only a duty, it is also a spiritual necessity for our prayer
fellowship with God. A heart that is filled with hatred, malice, or
resentment can never be a heart in which God lives and moves.

An interesting example of the relationship that exists between
right human relationships and effective prayer is found in an
unexpected place in the New Testament. The example must be
seen behind the lines of the story, but I am convinced that it is
there. As Paul and Barnabas prepared for their second missionary
journey, a sharp conflict arose between them over whether to
take Mark with them or not (Acts 15:36–39). These men, who
had so often experienced the leadership of God, were unable to
find it at this time. Why? Perhaps it was because each of them
was so adamant in his own opinion of the right course of action
that neither of them thought to seek the guidance of the Father.
Paul may have been the one most at fault, for he seems to have
failed to have the Christian spirit of love toward Mark. Perhaps
they failed to pray because they recognized the uselessness of
prayer while unable to find fellowship with each other. At any
rate, it would seem to me that we have an example of the truth
that our relationships with one another must be right or our
relationship with God in prayer cannot be effective.

Peter wrote to the Christian husbands concerning their relation
to their wives. The reason he gives for insisting that husbands
should "live considerately" with their wives is that their "prayers
may not be hindered" (I Peter 3:7). The teaching here seems to
be that the "sighs of the injured wife come between the husband's

prayer and God's hearing."[48] This same thought—that the cries of those whom we oppress or mistreat is a hindrance to prayer because they turn God's ear from us—is expressed by James. He says, "Behold, the wages of the laborers who mowed your fields, which you kept back by fraud, cry out; and the cries of the harvesters have reached the ears of the Lord of hosts" (James 5:4). The critical meaning of proper family relationships in prayer is also mentioned by Paul. He suggests that abstinence from sexual relationship be practiced only by mutual consent and that for a temporary season, "that you may devote yourselves to prayer" (I Cor. 7:5). The implication is that a disturbed family relationship will lead to the blocking of a prayer communion with God, either because God will not hear us or because we cannot achieve an attitude of true prayer.

Love of neighbor, of fellowmen, is essential to effective prayer. If we would desire to pray, we must be careful to maintain Christian relations in the church, in the home, and in the world. When these relations are disturbed, either through our own fault or through the fault of others, we must mend them before we can approach God as we should.

The third thing that is involved in being a practicing Christian is participation in the service of Christ. A presidential candidate once said, "I wish I had more supporters and fewer well-wishers." One difficulty with modern Christianity is that a large number of its "constituents" are mere "spectators" in the battle of the ages. They take no active part in the work of Christ; they hope that Christianity comes out ahead, but their policy is one of "wait and see" rather than "trust and obey."

The particular phrase that connects the necessity of active participation to effective prayer is "in my name." As Jesus faced the reality of the cross, he said to his disciples: "If you ask anything of the Father, he will give it to you in my name. Hitherto you have asked nothing in my name; ask, and you will receive, that your joy may be full" (John 16:23–24). In this way, Jesus opened to his followers a new way of prayer. "Hitherto" they had prayed as other Jews had prayed; now they are to pray as

Christians pray—in the name of Jesus. His cross and resurrection experience was to be the inauguration of God's new rule; it was to make clear that the way of approach to God was through the person of Jesus Christ. If we are to be men of effective prayer, we must understand what it means to pray in the name of Jesus; there are no limits to what we may ask and expect to receive if we pray "in his name."

"The name of Jesus" is not a magic formula to ensure the answer to all our petitions; it is not a sort of open sesame by which the treasures of heaven are opened to the clutching hands of men. It involves far more than a mere phrase that is used at the end of prayer to make it sound Christian. The itinerant Jewish exorcists found this out in Ephesus when they attempted to cast out an evil spirit in the name of Jesus. They had seen Paul do this. They came to believe that his power lay in his use of the "magic formula." So they "undertook to pronounce the name of the Lord Jesus over those who had evil spirits." Parroting Paul, they said, "I adjure you by the Jesus whom Paul preaches." The evil spirit answered them: "Jesus I know, and Paul I know; but who are you?" Following this, the man with the evil spirit attacked and mastered all of them, "so that they fled out of that house naked and wounded" (Acts 19:13–16). How different the experience of the Seventy, whom Jesus sent out in pairs. They returned, rejoicing, and said, "Lord, even the demons are subject to us in your name!" (Luke 10:17).

To use the name of Jesus with power demands that there be a reality behind the words. The Jewish exorcists sought to use them as a magic formula for selfish ends, and failed. The Seventy used them as the natural consequence of their position as the messengers of Christ, sent out by him, exercising his authority. They succeeded.

One writer has suggested that to ask "in the name of Jesus" is to ask on the basis of the merits of Christ. He illustrates his thought by a common experience of human life. When a man writes a check on a bank in which he has an account, his check is honored in his own name. If he writes one on a bank in which he has no deposit, the check will not be honored. However, if a friend who does have an account in that bank gives him a check to cash, the bank will honor it in the friend's name.[49] He applies his illustration by saying, "So it is when I go to the bank of heaven when I go to God in prayer. I have nothing deposited there, I have absolutely no credit there, and if I go in my own name I will get absolutely nothing; but Jesus Christ has unlimited credit in heaven, and he has granted to me the privilege of going to the bank with his name on my checks, and when I thus go, my prayers will be honored to any extent."[50]

This is a more Christian explanation than the supposition that "the name of Jesus" is a mere formula of power. However, it fails to explain the meaning of the phrase at one important point. What must be true of me before I can use the name of Jesus as an appeal in prayer? Jesus has not handed out a "power of attorney" to every Christian and told us to take advantage of the treasures of heaven without limitation. We cannot pray as if we had the "keys of the city" and every door had to open at our knock.

What does it mean? To ask in "Jesus' name" is to ask as his representative. Only as we take the place of a representative of Christ on earth, only as we live "in his name," only then can we pray in his name. This was suggested in the report of the Seventy that the demons were subject to them in the name of Jesus. The reason lay in the fact that Jesus had sent them out. They were his representatives. When they spoke, they had his "power of attorney" even among the fiends of hell. The same thing is true when we approach the throne of heaven in prayer; we can approach it with full assurance when we come as the representatives of the Lord Jesus Christ.

To illustrate, I have a position of some responsibility and authority in the school where I teach. The resources of the school are open to me up to a point. I may go to the business office and ask for a typewriter ribbon and my request will be granted. I have a secretary (at least sometimes) who works for me, writes my letters, and performs whatever tasks I may assign to her. If she went to the business office, she would have no status, no privilege of asking for supplies. Any request she made would be denied unless she made it in my name. If she asked in my name, the business manager, knowing that she is my secretary and assuming that she could be trusted, would grant her request to the same measure that he would grant mine if I made it in person.

This, I think, illustrates what must be true of anyone who would pray in the name of Jesus. He must be an accredited representative of Jesus; he must be involved in the service of Christ. This relation of life and prayer may be illustrated further by the examples of the prophets and of Jesus. The prophets "spoke in the name of the Lord" (James 5:10). This meant that their message was the message of God. They never introduced their message with the words, "I say unto you." Rather, they said, "God says." Jesus said of himself, "I have come in my Father's name, and you do not receive me; if another comes in his own name, him you will receive" (John 5:43). In another connection he claimed that the works which he did were done in the "Father's name" (John 10:25). What this meant for Jesus is expressed in his words to the disciples at Jacob's well, "My food is to do the will of him who sent me, and to accomplish his work" (John 4:34).

The idea of living in "the name of Jesus" is the regulative thought of the Christian life. The relation of the disciples to Christ is plainly stated in the words of the Master: "As the Father has sent me, even so I send you" (John 20:21). The new Testament makes much of this idea. Jesus said to his disciples, "He who receives you receives me, and he who receives me receives him who sent me" (Matt. 10:40). He taught that the church, when it gathers, ought to assemble in his name (Matt. 18:20). Paul's appeal to the Romans for their partnership in intercessory prayer was made in the name of Jesus (Rom. 15:30). He appealed to the Corinthians to seek unity of heart and mind, and his appeal was made in the name of Jesus (I Cor. 1:10). He declared that he had already passed judgment on the Corinthian sinner "in the name of the Lord Jesus" (I Cor. 5:4).

He gave instructions in "the name of our Lord Jesus Christ" to the Thessalonians (II Thess. 3:6). What was true of Paul should be true of every Christian. The admonition of the Scriptures is, "Whatever you do, in word or deed, do everything in the name of the Lord Jesus" (Col. 3:17).

The intent of Jesus' teaching that we pray "in his name" is not so much to point out a method of prayer but to define the way of life that ensures that we will have access to God. The promise of unlimited power through "prayer in his name" is joined to the promise of power in service. This relation is made clear in the first occurrence of the expression. "Truly, truly, I say to you, he who believes in me will also do the works that I do; and greater works than these will he do, because I go to the Father. Whatever you ask in my name, I will do it, that the Father may be glorified in the Son; if you ask anything in my name, I will do it." (John 14:12–14.)

Four things are to be noted in this passage. (1) The departure of Jesus involved his death and resurrection and the consequent coming of the Holy Spirit. But it involved more than this. It heralded the entrance of the disciples into their work as the messengers of God, the "salt of the earth," the "light of the world." Hitherto, they had been learners preparing for the coming task. Now graduation day had come. They had to begin their life as "ambassadors" of heaven. (2) Their work will be successful. It shakes our faith to read the promise of Jesus that they would do the same kind of works that he had done and even greater works than these. And this not only applies to the original Twelve. It is true of all who "believe." This whole passage is concerned with their work and its success. (3) Their work will not be successful because of their own strength. They will need the provision of heaven; without it they will be helpless. (4) Prayer "in the name of Jesus" is the method by which they will obtain the provision of heaven for the work of Christ.

The thought of this passage is not concerned primarily with answered prayer; it is concerned with responsibility. Plainly implied in all that Jesus said is the idea that answered prayer will come only when the responsibility to serve is accepted. There is no limit to what may be asked; there is a limit on who may ask it and why they may ask it. It is not to be asked for selfish pleasure, but for Christian service. It is to be asked by those who are deeply involved in the "work of faith" and the "labor of love." Others may ask, but they ask in vain. Prayer "in Jesus' name" means nothing unless we live "in Jesus name."

Effective prayer begins, then, with the person who prays, not with the method or conditions of prayer. "Your request is my command" is not said by God to every man. Before we can pray consistently with power and see the world and ourselves changed as a result of our prayer, we must be Christians, we must be practicing Christians, Christians who sincerely seek the life of righteousness, love, and service. Before we can enter the gates of prayer, our credentials must be in order.

But this does not end our responsibility. Not only must we be qualified to pray; we must pray in God's way. A study of the way to effective prayer must lead us to look at the requirements of faith and perseverance.

Faith—Synopsis

The New Testament presents faith as the one necessity for effective prayer by the committed Christian.

Faith, to lead to effective prayer, must be Christian faith. It must not be merely intellectual, nor can it be incomplete at this point.

Christian faith has four vitally related elements: believing, trusting, surrender, and fidelity.

Faith in the practice of prayer follows the same principles as faith in general, but it needs special application.

In prayer, faith includes the spirit of helplessness.

In prayer, faith includes sincerity. Sincerity means, negatively, that we do not pray to impress men. Positively, it means that we pray with a sincere desire to receive that for which we ask.

In prayer, faith includes discernment of God's will. We find out what God wants to give and we ask him for it. Methods of discerning the will of God include Bible study, observation of the circumstances of our life, and the leadership of the Holy Spirit.

In prayer, faith includes submission to the will of God. This means that we are willing for God to answer our petitions in his own way and that we are willing for him to use us in his answer.

In prayer, faith is expectant. Faith knows that no prayer is ever in vain.

VIII

Effective Prayer: Faith

The material included in this chapter is, as in many books on prayer, divided into several chapters and discussed under such titles as "conditions of answered prayer" or "hindrances to prayer." It has seemed to me, however, that helplessness, sincerity, discernment, submission, and expectancy are all included in Christian faith. If this is true, Christian faith includes all the elements that are necessary to ensure effective prayer on the part of that one who is qualified to pray.

It may be personal bias on my part that makes me refuse to think of faith, or anything else, as a "condition" of answered prayer. "Condition" suggests a contractual relationship in which one person promises to do something in return for the meeting of certain conditions or stipulations. The word lends itself to the conception of reward given in return for service rendered. I am aware that those who have written of "conditions" of answered prayer do not have this concept in mind, but it would seem best to avoid the danger by not using the term. At any cost, we must avoid making faith a "rule of prayer" which "resembles a magical prescription—like the rule of the ancient rabbi, . . . who knew that his prayer was heard whenever it was 'fluent in his mouth.' "[51]

There have been persons who, misunderstanding the meaning of faith and the promise of God, have felt that when they asked God for something, believing they would receive it, God was under obligation to deliver it. One woman is reported to have said, "I asked, fully expecting to get, and did not receive, so the promise failed."[52] This is by no means an uncommon conception, but it is contrary to the teachings of the New Testament. Any attempt that man might make to put God under obligations to grant his desire is unchristian.

It would seem better to think of faith as the "way" to effective prayer, a way in which the will of God is brought to pass in the life of the worshiper. The New Testament teaches that faith is essential to effective prayer; prayer without faith is futile. "If any of you lacks wisdom, let him ask God. . . . But let him ask in faith, with no doubting, for he who doubts . . . must not suppose that . . . [he] will receive anything from the Lord." (James 1:5-8.) The teaching of James in this passage is the reverse side of the teaching of Jesus that insists that the prayer of faith will be effective. "And whatever you ask in prayer, you will receive, if you have faith." (Matt. 21:22; cf. Mark 11:24.) James adds his testimony to the effectiveness of the prayer of faith in a specific instance by saying, "The prayer of faith will save the sick man" (James 5:15). It would seem to follow that if faith guarantees effective prayer, nothing else is essential to it. If lack of faith makes prayer futile, nothing else will make it effective. Therefore, all the essential elements that constitute a way to effective prayer are included in the Christian conception of faith.

Notice that we say the "Christian conception of faith." There are conceptions of faith that are not Christian; some of these are mentioned in the New Testament. One kind of faith that falls short of Christian faith is that which is merely intellectual. "You believe that God is one; you do well. Even the demons believe— and shudder." (James 2:19.) Luther, as is well known, condemned the letter of James as a "straw" epistle because he thought its discussion of faith contradicted that of Paul. As a matter of fact, James does not contradict Paul; he complements him. James was dealing with a group of people who believed that they had faith simply because they were orthodox in their theology. Their faith made no vital difference in their lives; it did not lead to surrender to God nor to concern for their brothers in Christ. Such faith was futile. "What does it profit, my brethren, if a man says he has faith but has not works? Can his faith save him?" (James 2:14.) James does not belittle faith; he does not want less faith. James "wants faith to be the real thing and to result in the entire dedication of life."[53] Such faith as James condemns could never be the way to effective prayer; it is not Christian faith at all.

Another kind of faith mentioned in the New Testament that falls short of Christian faith is an incomplete faith. "Many believed in his name when they saw the signs which he did." (John 2:23.) That the faith mentioned in this passage was incomplete is shown by the fact that "Jesus did not trust himself to them" (v. 24). He recognized that their faith was not true faith. Wherein did it come short? The clue is found in the next chapter. Nicodemus seems to have been one of those who believed in him because he saw the signs. When he approached Jesus, he said, "Rabbi, we know that you are a teacher come from God; for no one can do these signs that you do, unless God is with him" (John 3:2). Observe the doctrinal content of this faith. It led Nicodemus to say that Jesus was a "teacher come from God." But Jesus was far more than this; he was eternal Son of God, the Savior of the world. In other cases, the belief of the people, though it accepted the Messiahship of Jesus, did not discern the Kingdom of God as a spiritual reality. When Jesus had fed the five thousand, the people said, "This is indeed the prophet who is to come into the world!" (John 6:14). In this case, the theology is higher, it seems, but the faith is still incomplete. "Perceiving then that they were about to come and take him by force to make him king, Jesus withdrew again to the hills by himself." (V. 15.) Again, Jesus could not trust himself to them. "He could not trust them and their program for him [of a political kingdom], because they had not trusted him and his program for them [of a spiritual salvation]."[54] Incomplete faith can never be the way to effective prayer.

Before we can understand the way to effective prayer, we must understand the Christian conception of faith. Before we can understand how faith operates in prayer, we must understand its meaning in the whole of the Christian life.

Christian faith has four vitally related elements: believing, trusting, surrender, and fidelity. Faith is incomplete when any one of these is lacking or incomplete. Though some passages on faith emphasize one or the other of these elements as primary in the thought of the writer, all are always involved in a secondary way when faith is thought to be Christian in its quality.

One important element of faith is believing; this is not the whole of faith, but it is an essential element. Since faith in the New Testament is always thought of as adherence to a Person, the person of God in Christ Jesus, it is natural that faith must include something that one believes about that Person. Christian faith always has a doctrinal content; it can never be divorced from theology. This is what saves faith from being a "blind leap in the dark." In John's Gospel, the verb "believe" (Greek, *pisteuō*) is used over ninety times. Sixty-four times the object of the verb is expressed in the context. In thirty of these instances, faith is believing that something is true or that some person is trustworthy. The essential doctrinal content of Christian faith is seen in the fact that "faith" came to be a synonym for the contents of Christian theology. "I found it necessary to write appealing to you to contend for the faith which was once for all delivered to the saints." (Jude 3.) This is a use of the word that is very rare in the New Testament but has come to be rather common in Christian usage. However, it needs to be stressed that doctrinal correctness is never taught to be adequate. Believing something about God calls for action. We might say that believing is the foundation of faith. No enduring structure of faith can be built without the foundation, but the foundation alone is useless.

Proper belief naturally leads one to trust himself to the saving power and mercy of Christ. Faith is the prisoner standing at the judgment bar, knowing he is guilty and deserves condemnation, but throwing "himself on the mercy of the court." Faith is "the acceptance of the gospel message concerning Jesus Christ, and the committal of one's self for salvation to him or to God as revealed in him."[55] This element of faith is a central emphasis of Paul's great doctrinal epistles. "For we hold that a man is justified by

faith apart from works of law." (Rom. 3:28.) The phrase "apar
from works of law" means that faith is the complete committe
of self to the mercy of Christ. No claims are made. Legalisti
works may exist, but they are cast aside. The sinner, realizin
himself to be without merit, pleads for mercy. He does this, o
course, because he believes that God is a God of mercy. Th
Christian gospel assures him that this is true.

Faith does not end with trust; it goes on to surrender to th
Lordship of Christ over one's life. It is never the thought of th
New Testament that a sinner can simply confess his sins, tru
Christ to save him, and then go his own way without regard t
the will of God. Faith recognizes that sin deserves to be punishe
and seeks forgiveness; it also recognizes that sin ought to be re
pudiated and seeks the effective rule of God. The first questio
that Paul asked on the Damascus road after he had recognize
the heavenly Voice as that of Jesus of Nazareth was, "What sha
I do, Lord?" This question set the pattern for his life of faith. A
he neared the end of life, he could say, "I do not account my lif
of any value nor as precious to myself, if only I may accomplis
my course and the ministry which I received from the Lord Jesu
to testify to the gospel of the grace of God" (Acts 20:24). H
most-used title for Jesus was "Lord"; his favorite description o
himself was *"Paulos doulos Iēsou Christou,"* literally, "Paul,
bondslave of Jesus Christ" (cf. Rom. 1:1). He described th
"word" of faith as being, "If you confess with your lips that Jest
is Lord and believe in your heart that God raised him from th
dead, you will be saved" (Rom. 10:9). Notice that the Revise
Standard Version "Confess . . . that Jesus is Lord" correctly tran
lates the Greek in this verse. The King James Version has "Co
fess . . . the Lord Jesus," which weakens, if it does not destro
the force of the expression. We conclude, then, that surrende
the spirit of obedience, is an essential part of Christian faith.

But faith is more than a beginning; it is the creation of
permanent bond between man and God. The surrender that take
place in a moment of time must be lived out in a life of fidelit
The bonds of matrimony that are assumed at a wedding are su
posed to last until "death do us part." The bond of union estab

lished at the moment of our acknowledgment of the Lordship of Christ over our lives must last for eternity. "Faith" in this sense is said to last forever, to be a part of our heavenly existence (I Cor. 13:13). It is certainly to be a continuing part of our earthly existence. This essential reality of faith is stressed in the book of Hebrews. "Faith" there, in most cases, should be rendered by "faithfulness" or "fidelity." "We are not of those who shrink back and are destroyed, but of those who have faith and keep their souls." (Heb. 10:39.) By this expression, the writer of Hebrews says that a faith that does not continue is not true faith. A building blown down by the first wind is not a good building; in a sense, it is no building at all. So it is with faith. If a man turns away from Christ, it means that he has never truly turned to him.

What we have said so far only sketches the meaning of faith in the Christian life as a whole without defining how faith is related to the practice of prayer. The essential elements of faith are the same in relation to prayer as elsewhere, but they call for special applications. It would seem to me that the material for study in the New Testament would indicate five essentials of the "prayer of faith" that would not only save the sick but accomplish the purpose of God in the life of the one who prays.

In prayer, the spirit of helplessness is a part of faith. Faith in God presupposes lack of faith in self. An example of the futility of prayer without a spirit of helplessness and of the effectiveness of prayer with it is seen in the parable of the Pharisee and publican (Luke 18:9–14). Luke tells us that the parable was told "to some who trusted in themselves that they were righteous" and as a result "despised others." The characters of the story were chosen deliberately. The Pharisees were those among the Jews who felt themselves superior to all others. They exercised themselves to keep the law and the rabbinic traditions in hope that they could win the approval of God for their lives. To Jesus, their prayers were a mockery. They did not come to God as men with desperate need, relying completely on the grace and power of God. They came as men who felt no need, full of pride. The prayer that Jesus put into the mouth of the Pharisee is no doubt a caricature of all Pharisaic praying. "God, I thank thee that I am not like other men, extortioners, unjust, adulterers, or even like this tax collector. I fast twice a week, I give tithes of all that I get." In effect, he said: "God, look at me; I am one of your prize children. I need no help; I am self-sufficient."

The tax collector represented a class of men who had given up in their religious quest. They had "sold out" to the Romans and become hirelings of the oppressors. Probably not many of them ever prayed. When they did, they would have prayed as this one did. The prayer that Jesus put in his mouth is a model of desperate helplessness. He stood afar off, refused to presume to lift his eyes toward heaven, kept on beating his breast, and cried out, "God, be merciful to me the sinner" (my translation).

What was the result? Jesus said, "I tell you, this man [i.e., the tax collector] went down to his house justified rather than the other [i.e., the Pharisee]." We may suppose that the Pharisee went down to his house "satisfied"; he had prayed; he had performed his religious duty; it never occurred to him that God was not pleased. But God was not satisfied; his prayer had been in vain. The tax collector, however, had been heard; he was "justified" before God; his prayer had been effective.

So it always is with prayer. The prayer of faith begins when the Christian feels himself to be helpless. It is "the poor in spirit" who inherit "the kingdom of heaven" (Matt. 5:3). Just as the mother learns to distinguish between her baby's cry that expresses anger and that which expresses fear or need, God distinguishes between the cries of his children for help. When help is really needed, when weakness is really consciously recognized, the answer of God is as swift as the care of the mother.

When the disciples cried out in fright, "Teacher, do you not care if we perish?" (Mark 4:38), Jesus calmed the sea. When the father of the epileptic cried out in despair, "I believe; help my unbelief!" (Mark 9:24), Jesus healed his son. So it is with the Father. When the children realize their own helplessness and cry out for help, help is always near. It would seem to me that the spirit of helplessness is essential to effective prayer. It is an element in faith when faith is related to prayer.

In prayer, sincerity is a part of faith. The man who prays must
be sincere in his quest for the will of God to be done in his life.
The runner who takes his eyes from the goal to see how others
are running invariably loses the race. When the man who prays
is concerned about the impression he is making on men, his
prayer is vain. The first meaning of sincerity in prayer is negative.
Men must not pray in pretense. Prayer must not be a display of
piety. Jesus spoke of those "who devour widows' houses" and "for
a pretense make long prayers" (Mark 12:40; Luke 20:47). Need
we say that such prayers mean nothing to God? They may be
effective in fooling men; they could never be effective in causing
the will of God to be done.

It seems that this would be a self-evident matter, that it would
need no mention. Yet Jesus took seriously the danger that prayer
might be insincere. He recognized that there is a real temptation
to be insincere in religion. He said, "Beware of practicing your
piety before men in order to be seen by them" (Matt. 6:1). Jesus
would not have cried "wolf" when there was no danger. "Beware"
is a word that expresses the need for constant vigilance against
danger. Jesus discussed this danger in relation to almsgiving,
fasting, and prayer. With reference to prayer, he said: "When
you pray, you must not be like the hypocrites; for they love to
stand and pray in the synagogues and at the street corners, that
they may be seen by men. Truly, I say to you, they have their
reward" (v. 5).

Jesus gave some practical advice to help his disciples avoid the
temptation to insincerity. He said, "When you pray, go into your
room and shut the door and pray to your Father who is in secret;
and your Father who sees in secret will reward you" (Matt. 6:6).
This is still good advice. A person is far less likely to pray super-
ficially when he prays in secret than when he prays in public.
However, even secret prayer is no guarantee against ostentatious-
ness in religion. One may pray in secret and then "let the secret
out" in order to impress men. Nor, on the other hand, is public
prayer to be wholly prohibited. The temptation here may be
greater. Even the Christian minister, in leading his congregation

in prayer, may use prayer as a means of preaching or seek to in press the congregation with the beauty of his diction. Or he m. use public prayer with sincerity and add to the richness of publ worship and to the strength of his congregation's Christian e perience.

The testing point must always be the motivation of our hear Either in public or in private, the object of prayer is to seek con munion with God, to throw ourselves upon his mercy, to ope the "door of our need" to his grace. When this motivation ca tures and controls prayer, it may be practiced in any place an be effective as a means of God's grace in our lives. "Since pray is essentially a quest, no response can be expected if the quest not wholeheartedly and utterly sincere."[56]

The negative side of sincerity is to avoid any effort to impre men. The positive side is to really want that for which we as Listen to Paul. He says: "I am speaking the truth in Christ, am not lying; my conscience bears me witness in the Holy Spir that I have great sorrow and unceasing anguish in my heart. F I could wish that I myself were accursed and cut off from Chr for the sake of my brethren, my kinsmen by race" (Rom. 9:1– Can anyone doubt the sincerity of Paul's prayer for Israel's salv tion? He says, "Brethren, my heart's desire and prayer to God f them is that they may be saved" (Rom. 10:1). When we pray, v must be sure that we are willing to receive the answer to o prayer; we must be sincere in our request.

The answer to prayer is not always as desirable as it mig seem. We may pray for patience and find that God answers giving us suffering. We may pray for the world to be saved an find ourselves ministering to lepers. We may pray for God's w to be done and find ourselves on a cross. The answers of God prayer do not always come in the way that men expect; som times they cost the man who receives God's blessings what m seem a terrible price. This need not surprise us. Character can molded only in the crucible of experience. The virtues of Chr can be given only to those who want them sincerely enough receive them at any cost.

Luke tells of three men who wanted to be followers of Chri

One was discouraged when he learned of the poverty of Jesus; one wanted to wait until he had buried his father; the other asked for permission to say farewell to those in his house (Luke 9:57–61). The comment of Jesus was, "No one who puts his hand to the plow and looks back is fit for the kingdom of God" (v. 62). Their request to be his followers was rejected because it was not sincere; they were not willing to follow at any cost.

So it is with prayer. Unless we sincerely desire that for which we ask, we ask in vain. Too often, we want the blessing without the necessity of following the road that we must follow to receive it. I am often persuaded that my students want to know Greek, but few of them are willing to learn it. They ask me to teach them. I cannot answer because their request is not sincere. Simon Magus wanted to have power to confer the Holy Spirit on others, power like that of Peter and John. But he wanted it without the discipline that had given it to them; he wanted to buy it with money. Is it any wonder that Peter condemned his request and called it "wickedness" (cf. Acts 8:14–23)?

Prayer then must be sincere. It must be directed toward God without any thought for the impact it may make on men. It must sincerely desire the blessings asked. This is not something apart from faith; it is a part of faith.

In prayer, faith includes discernment of God's will. If the purpose of prayer is to accomplish the will of God in the life of the one who prays and in the world through his prayer, effective prayer must be in harmony with God's will. The praying one must discover the desire of God and make that his prayer. The unbeliever might scoff at this concept of prayer. He might say, "Prayer is not much of anything if all it means is finding out what God wants to do and asking him to do it." The unbeliever is inclined to think of prayer as a means of manipulating God, of using God. He reflects in his thinking the pagan idea that the aim of religion is to bring the deity worshiped under the control of the worshiper.

The Christian has rejected this idea of religion. He believes that God is to be worshiped, not manipulated; God is to be followed, not controlled. He believes not only in the power of God but also in the love and wisdom of God. To believe in the love of God is to believe that what God desires for us is always our good. To believe in the wisdom of God is to believe that what God desires for us is always the best for us ultimately. Solomon, it is said, asked for wisdom when God said, "Ask what I shall give you" (I Kings 3:5). God was pleased with the choice of Solomon and granted his request. Solomon had discerned the desire of God for his life and made that his prayer. His prayer as a result was effective. One Christian has suggested that if God should come to him with a similar proposal, a proposal to give him a special gift, he would say, "Dear God, *you* choose. I choose what *you* choose."[57]

One essential, then, in effective prayer is discernment, and since faith is considered the one essential way to effective prayer in the New Testament, faith must include discernment. But how is a person to know what God's will is when he prays? There is no absolute standard by which this may be accomplished. No sincere Christian could ever be dogmatic in saying that this or that thing for which he prays is God's will. Most of us must always end our petitions with a conditional clause: "if this be thy will." Yet there are ways in which we may discern the will of God, ways which faith should follow in the act of prayer.

One way of discerning God's will is through the study of the Bible, especially of the New Testament. We may take it as assured that whatever is revealed there as God's will for all Christians is his will for us. To illustrate, the New Testament teaches that all Christians are to be witnesses for Christ. There is no evidence of any exceptions. Therefore every Christian may pray that God will help him to become a witness and know that his prayer is in harmony with the will of God. However, just to pray for this in a general way is not enough. Prayer becomes effective when we ask for help to witness to someone in particular, somewhere in particular, and in a particular manner. The New Testament does not teach me the particulars of my prayer for aid in witnessing. How, then, shall I discern the will of God in reference to these particulars?

One way to discern the will of God is to look at the circumstances of my own life. The ancient dictum, "Whatever your hand finds to do, do it with your might" (Eccl. 9:10), often reveals to the eye of faith the will of God. The exercise of good judgment is a spiritual exercise. To illustrate with reference to my witnessing, if I have an unsaved child, surely it is God's will for me to witness to my child. I can pray with assurance that it is God's will that God will help me through my example, my love, and my precepts to lead my own to a knowledge of Christ.

A Biblical example of discerning the will of God through observation of circumstances may be found in Paul's letter to the Philippian church. Paul faced the possibility of death and welcomed it as a pathway to glory; he recognized the possibility of continued life and service and shrank from it. "I am hard pressed between the two. My desire is to depart and be with Christ, for that is far better. But to remain in the flesh is more necessary on your account." (Phil. 1:23–24.) That Paul's observation of the circumstances led him to see that his continued life and ministry was God's desire for him and that his prayer was brought into harmony with God's desire is shown by his statement: "I trust in the Lord that shortly I myself shall come also" (Phil. 2:24). Observation will give me assurance of God's will in a great number of cases, but it will not always suffice. Faith must have more help in discerning God's will.

This help is found in the ministry of the Holy Spirit in relation to prayer. The prayer of faith is a prayer "in the Spirit." "Pray in the Holy Spirit" is one of the closing admonitions of the writer of Jude (v. 20). Paul admonished the Ephesians, "Pray at all times in the Spirit, with all prayer and supplication" (Eph. 6:18). "Likewise the Spirit helps us in our weakness; for we do not know how to pray as we ought, but the Spirit himself intercedes for us with sighs too deep for words. And he who searches the hearts of men knows what is the mind of the Spirit, because the Spirit intercedes for the saints according to the will of God." (Rom. 8:26–27.)

A study of the Romans passage indicates how the Spirit helps faith discern the will of God in prayer. There is something about prayer that we do not know. Just what is not known is a subject of debate among scholars. We may reject, I think, as unworthy of the Christian, let alone of Paul, the suggestion that this reminiscent of the Gnostic idea of a secret formulation that gives us access to God. "It is certain that Paul does not mean what the Gnostics meant; for him, prayer is no formula, nor are men saved by repeating unintelligible words."[58] Nor is the explanation of this passage by Barth satisfying. He seems to say that the prayer in mind is the prayer for salvation, a prayer that we do not know how to pray. Therefore, the Father makes himself our intercessor and "utters for us that ineffable groaning, . . . so that he will accept what he himself has to offer."[59] Rhys insists that we do know the proper object of petition—adoption—since it has been revealed to us. The weakness lies in the manner of prayer. "We lack the sincerity, the singleness of purpose, that should be ours."[60]

It would seem that the object of prayer is just the place where human weakness occurs. The expression, "We do not know how to pray as we ought" is an attempt to translate the Greek expression *katho dei* ("according as it is necessary"). The necessity involved is usually, in the New Testament, related to the necessity or obligation that is involved in the redemptive purpose of God. In general, we do know that we ought to pray for the perfection of our salvation. But we do not know what we should pray for in the light of the immediate need of our lives. "We know the end which is common to all prayers, but not what is necessary at each crisis of need in order to enable us to attain this end."[61] We find something of an example of this dilemma in the experience of Jesus as he faced the coming of the cross and said: "Now is my soul troubled. And what shall I say? 'Father, save me from this hour'? No, for this purpose I have come to this hour" (John 12:27). There are many crisis points in the Christian life where the exact prayer that it is necessary for us to utter in order to achieve God's will in our life is beyond our knowledge.

But how does the Spirit help us in our infirmity at this point? The expression, "The Spirit himself intercedes for us," is subject to misunderstanding. It would seem to suggest that the Christian is passive in the whole transaction, that he stands aside and lets the Holy Spirit act in his behalf. The difficulty arises from the nature of the case. We must always be careful to distinguish the action of the Spirit from the action of our own spirit; these must never be confused. But distinguishing often leads to a separation that does not do justice to the facts of the case. The Spirit does not guide us apart from the exercise of our own consciousness and power. "He guides us rather by indwelling, by stimulating and directing our powers."[62] Thus, "the sighs that are too deep for words" are our sighs created within us by the action of the Holy Spirit and become the expression of our own hearts as they become instruments of the "mind of the Spirit."

Admittedly, this discussion ends in a mystery to the non-Christian. The whole matter of Spirit's leadership in prayer can be understood only in the light of experience. What man is there who makes a practice of sincere and earnest prayer who has not come face to face with a crisis of life in which he knew not how to pray? In such a time, he has thrown himself upon the mercy of God and sought to communicate with him. Mysteriously, yet wonderfully, in such a time has he felt the nearness of God through his Spirit, has groaned within himself, unable to express the deep desires of his heart, and yet has known in some way that God understood and answered. This is what Paul is talking about in this passage; it is born out of his own experience.

Another passage of like meaning in relation to social or corporate prayer is found in Matt. 18:19–20: "Again I say to you, if two of you agree on earth about anything they ask, it will be done for them by my Father in heaven. For where two or three are gathered in my name, there am I in the midst of them." These two verses are often separated and misunderstood as a result of their separation. The picture that Jesus draws in them is of the church, the congregation, even though it consists of only two people. They meet "in the name of Christ" to consider their mission in the world and to pray. But they are not alone; Jesus is there. He moves within them to "symphonize" their prayer. They reach agreement, not on the basis of human discussion and desire, but because of his presence in the Holy Spirit. They "agree" on what they shall ask of the Father. Because their prayer is Spirit-led, they have the assurance that it is the will of God and it will be granted.

Discerning the will of God and making that will our prayer assures us of the effectiveness of our praying. "This is the confidence which we have in him, that if we ask anything according to his will he hears us. And if we know that he hears us in whatever we ask, we know that we have obtained the requests made of him." (I John 5:14-15.)

In prayer, faith includes submission to the will of God. Much of what we have said in relation to discerning the will of God would apply equally well under this heading. We are not likely to discern until we are willing to submit. This only illustrates the fact that our total discussion involves one subject rather than a number of them. We distinguish the various elements of faith in relation to prayer only that we may come to understand more fully what faith in prayer means. However, it will be in order to notice that submission to God's will involves two things: a willingness for God to answer our petition in his way and a willingness for God to answer our petition through our participation.

An example of willingness for God to answer a petition in his own way is found in Paul's prayer concerning the thorn in his flesh (II Cor. 12:7-9). Paul's own desire was to be rid of the "cursed thing." In the communion of prayer, he came to see that God's desire was to give him grace to live an overcoming life in spite of it. When he was convinced of this, Paul exclaimed, "I will all the more gladly boast of my weaknesses, that the power of Christ may rest upon me."

So it should be with us in prayer. God's will may be to answer our petition, but to answer it in some way other than that which we have anticipated or desired. When we understand this, faith submits. It welcomes the way of God and rejoices in the answer of his grace. We may pray for wealth and God will answer by giving us grace to live in poverty. We may pray for health and God will answer by giving us power to live a radiant life in a diseased body. Faith does not question the will of God; it does not rebel and refuse the answer given. It submits and rejoices in his love.

An example of submission to the will of God in his desire to answer prayer through our own participation is found, I think, in the story of Philip and the Ethiopian eunuch (Acts 8:26–40). "An angel of the Lord said to Philip, 'Rise and go toward the south to the road that goes down from Jerusalem to Gaza.' This is a desert road. And he rose and went." (Vs. 26–27.) Behind this experience must lie an experience of petition. We may well imagine that Philip was praying for the leadership of God. No doubt, what he had in mind was leadership in more effective ways of conducting the very successful revival campaign in Samaria. God answered his petition, but in a way wholly unexpected. To leave the city of Samaria with its crowds of eager listeners and go to a desert road would seem preposterous to men. Philip recognized it as the will of God. He saw that it involved his own action. He went. When he came to the road, the caravan of the eunuch was passing along. "The Spirit said to Philip, 'Go up and join this chariot.' So Philip ran to him." (Vs. 29–30.) Again, faith submits and acts in obedience to the will of God.

Another example of submission to the will of God is the story of Peter's ministry to Cornelius (Acts, ch. 10). While the messengers of Cornelius approached the city, "Peter went up on the housetop to pray" (v. 9). In his communion of prayer, his own racial (or perhaps better, religious) prejudice was called into question by the vision from heaven. When the messengers arrived, Peter recognized their request as the will of God. Peter answered in faith by submitting and going with them to preach the gospel to Cornelius and his household.

So it must always be with faith when we pray. God's answer to our petition may involve our own action. It may lead us to experiences and places that are unexpected and undesirable from a human standpoint. But faith submits to the will of God. Faith is willing to "put feet to its prayers." At no other place is the relation between "praying in faith" and faith as a Christian virtue more clear than here.

In prayer, faith is expectant. There is an old story of a hungry couple who decided to ask God to give them bread. In order to make the prayer real, they put an empty bread pan in a lighted oven and prayed for an hour that God would fill it with bread. At the end of the time, the oven was opened and the pan was found to be empty still. The man said, "I knew all the time that nothing would happen." Whatever else may be said about this prayer, it was certainly not a prayer that expected an answer.

Faith does expect an answer. James insists that the man who prays for wisdom will receive nothing unless he asks "in faith, with no doubting" (James 1:6). Jesus taught that we would receive whatever we ask in prayer if we believe that we have received it (Mark 11:24). Expectancy of an answer is not the whole of faith, as we have noticed, but it is a vital part of it. When we have prayed and are assured within our heart that what we have asked is in God's will, when we have prayed with submission, we may and should expect results. Paul prayed for rescue. He was assured that God would save the people on his ship. He began to act immediately as if the rescue was assured. He expected the answer.

But what of those times when we have not reached the assurance which it is our right to reach in prayer? Even then, the man of faith expects results. He may not know what the results will be, but he knows that God answers prayer. He knows that he has prayed with faith; he knows that his prayer will not be in vain.

Faith, then, for the man of faith, is the way to effective prayer. There is nothing else that is needed to ensure the effectiveness of our prayers in accomplishing the will of God in our life and in the life of the world except one thing. That one thing is that we actually practice praying, that we pray with perseverance.

Persevering in Prayer—Synopsis

The ideal of the New Testament is that prayer should be a continuous, habitual practice of the Christian life. Perseverance is to be perseverance in prayer, not in *a* prayer.

There are, however, certain petitions which it is proper to repeat, but never with the spirit of importunity.

The reason for "unanswered petitions" lies either in the fact that some petitions contradict our higher desires or in the fact that God desires to give us better blessings than we ask for.

Delay in answering prayer only means that God's time for giving does not always coincide with our time for asking. However, we may perceive that God has granted our request and live with the expectancy of receiving it in God's time.

Struggle in prayer is not struggle with God but with ourselves.

Effective Prayer: Persevering in Prayer

The ideal of prayer presented in the New Testament is that of continuous fellowship and communion with God in all the circumstances of life. There is no indication that prayer was ever meant to be a "court of last resort" when the troubles of life become so great that man is forced to appeal to God. Prayer is not to be an occasional experience such as buying a new car; it is to be a constant experience such as breathing. Prayer should be persistent in the sense that it is a continuous and habitual practice of life, not in the sense that we determine what we want and continue to hound God for it until he yields to our entreaties.

A discussion of persistence in prayer, because of the material for study in the New Testament as well as because of the misunderstanding of what it means to persist in prayer, must consider the following subjects: (1) the ideal of prayer in the New Testament, which is stated by Paul, "Pray constantly" (I Thess. 5:17), (2) the place that "importunity" plays in the success of our prayer life, (3) valid "continuing petitions in prayer," (4) the place that "unanswered prayers" play in our prayer life, (5) the experience of "delayed" results, and (6) the role of "struggle" in prayer.

Let us begin our consideration of the New Testament ideal of prayer as a continuing, habitual practice of life with our greatest example, Jesus Christ. One passage that underlines the fact that prayer was a habit of life for Jesus is found in the statement that Jesus "continued his practice of retiring to lonely places and praying" (Luke 5:16, my translation). The Greek form used in this statement is the periphrastic imperfect, which is the most emphatic way in Greek of stressing an action as durative and continuous. Many other passages in our Gospel records tell of the withdrawal of Jesus for a season of prayer, sometimes lasting the whole night through. We must not suppose, however, that Jesus prayed only when he was away from the crowd. He could call out unto the Father, while surrounded by people, as he approached the tomb of Lazarus (John 11:41-42), as well as in the throng of the Temple crowds when the Greeks sought to see him (John 12:27-30). All the material that we have about the prayer life of Jesus reveals that he was the perfect embodiment of the ideal of a habitual life of prayer. If we are to pray effectively, it would seem that we must seek to emulate him in this respect.

The records that we have of the prayer life of Paul are for the most part autobiographical; it is surprising how often the idea of continuous prayer is expressed in them. He writes to the Romans that he makes mention of them in his prayers "without ceasing" (Rom. 1:9). He tells the Philippians that he thanks God for them whenever he remembers them and "always" in every prayer makes petition for them (Phil. 1:3-4). He tells the Colossians that he "always" thanks God for them when he prays for them, (Col. 1:3). He reminds the Thessalonians that he "always" gives thanks to God for them, "constantly mentioning" them in his prayers (I Thess. 1:2-3), and insists that he prayed "earnestly night and day" for the privilege of coming and helping them in their Christian growth (I Thess. 3:10). He claims that he strives "greatly" for all those churches which have not seen his face in the flesh, an expression that, though it does not explicitly mention prayer, certainly implies continuation in it (Col. 2:1-2). What Paul has said about himself received confirmation from the writer of The Acts, who mentions many experiences of Paul in prayer, one when he took leave from the elders of Ephesus. It is said that "when he had spoken thus, he knelt down and prayed with them all" (Acts 20:36). The naturalness of this note suggests strongly that this was his habit and created no surprise in the minds of his companions.

What Paul did in following the example of Jesus in continuing prayer, others did also. Our knowledge of the prayer life of the New Testament Christians is, naturally, very limited; it would be as impossible as it is unnecessary to call the roll of the men of God in the first century and prove by specific statements that they practiced the ideal of continuous prayer. One example may be taken as representative of the more or less "unknowns" of the New Testament. "Epaphras, who is one of yourselves, a servant of Christ Jesus, greets you, always remembering you earnestly in his prayers." (Col. 4:12.) "Remembering you earnestly" is perhaps too mild a translation for the Greek here which really pictures prayer as a conflict and struggle. However, for our immediate subject, we are interested only in the fact that he prayed "always" for them, an expression that again emphasizes the ideal of prayer as a continuous practice of life. When we turn to the teachings of the New Testament, the ideal of habitual prayer is, if possible, even more prominent than in the example of prayer. Matthew introduces the teaching of Jesus on prayer in the Sermon on the Mount with the statement, "When you pray" (Matt. 6:5). Notice that it is not, "If you pray" but, "When you pray." The Greek particle behind the expression is one that could as well be translated, "Whenever you pray." The thought of Jesus seems to be that discipleship carries with the natural concomitant of continuing prayer. There is no doubt that disciples will pray. They must be instructed in how to pray. This thought is carried farther in the command and promise of Jesus, "Keep on asking and you will keep on receiving" (Luke 11:9, my translation). The present tenses in the Greek are often overlooked by the translators, but they are there and represent the action as continuous and habitual. Connected with the parable of the unjust judge is the application that Jesus made of it: "And he told them a parable, to the effect that they ought always to pray and not lose heart" (Luke 18:1).

The emphasis of Jesus on continuity in prayer characterizes the teachings of the epistles also. Paul admonishes the Colossians, "Continue steadfastly in prayer" (Col. 4:2). He tells the Thessalonians, "Pray constantly, give thanks in all circumstances; for this is the will of God in Christ Jesus for you" (I Thess. 5:17-18).

He suggests to the Philippians that rather than worry about the problems of life, they should "in everything by prayer and supplication with thanksgiving" let their "requests be made known to God" (Phil. 4:6). He admonishes the Ephesians, "Pray at all times in the Spirit, with all prayer and supplication" (Eph. 6:18). Impressive indeed is the constant emphasis of Paul in his letters upon the necessity of praying "always," "without ceasing," "steadfastly," etc. If I Timothy was written by Paul, we have still another indication of his thought that prayer should be a continuing practice of life. He describes the real widow, the kind who is worthy of support by the church, as one who has "set her hope on God and continues in supplications and prayers night and day" (I Tim. 5:5).

What Paul stresses is stressed also in other New Testament writings. James says: "Is any one among you suffering? Let him pray. Is any cheerful? Let him sing praise" (James 5:13). This passage teaches that there is an appropriate kind of prayer for every circumstance of life, petition in time of suffering, praise in time of rejoicing. Thus prayer should be a constant practice, though its form may vary with the circumstances of life. The writer of Hebrews says, "Through him then let us continually offer up a sacrifice of praise to God, that is, the fruit of lips that acknowledge his name" (Heb. 13:15), and admonishes the readers, using the present tense of continuous action, "Pray for us" (v. 18).

To those who have a picture of prayer as an exercise in which the Christian withdraws to a lonely place, kneels, and addresses words to God, the ideal of continuous prayer seems impossible to attain. Indeed it is. Who is there who has not, with the notion that he should pray continuously, decided that he will spend a single hour in prayer? When we do this, we soon find that we have run out of things to say. If we cannot pray continuously for a single hour, how can we pray continuously throughout life? The answer to this very pertinent question is not found by exegesis of the New Testament. Negatively, we may be sure that continuous prayer does not mean that we are to be in the act of addressing God continuously. Neither Jesus nor Paul did this. Much of their time was spent in preaching, teaching, and other forms of service to men. A suggestion may be found in the brief ejaculations of Jesus at the grave of Lazarus and in the Temple, which were mentioned above. Many men of prayer have stressed the value of such short ejaculations in the course of the daily life when a person may, in the presence of difficulty, simply cry out as he moves to solve that difficulty: "Help me, Lord." Or, when faced with a blessing, he may say, "Thank you, Lord." Perhaps more to the point is the suggestion that continuous prayer combines many types of prayer into a whole. It would involve seasons of prayer in the quiet place when we address God in prayer; it would involve the regular and habitual offering of thanks to God when we sit down to eat; it would involve the periodic ejaculation of thanksgiving or calls for help in the course of the daily life; perhaps even more vital, it would involve the creation and maintaining of a consciousness of God's presence in all the circumstances of life, a consciousness that would result in a continuing communion in our subconscious self even when our conscious mind is occupied with the course of life's experiences.

One might well ask why it is so important that prayer be continuous. The answer must lie in a number of directions. Perhaps the primary one is that our spiritual life is renewed and refreshed only as it experiences a continuous fellowship with God. Just as breathing is essential to the continued purification of our blood, so prayer is an essential to the continued purification of our souls. Another answer may lie in the fact that skill in prayer is developed, as in other realms of life, only through constant practice. The man who does not pray as a habit of life may find that he cannot pray in the crises of life. Every pastor has undoubtedly had a parishioner ask to be prayed for. He has responded with a willingness to do so and with a suggestion that the man pray for himself. How often has the reply come, "I don't know how to pray." Such ignorance of prayer is inexcusable in a Christian. The final answer may lie in the thought that neglect of prayer is a form of insult to God. If God is our God, if he is the most important reality of life, how can we neglect our communion with him? Surely continuous prayer is an essential element in our worship and life, a factor that must not be neglected or ignored.

This does not mean that one who has not prayed habitually is shut out from the throne of grace. The goodness of God is inexpressibly great, and we may be sure that God will hear the cry of despair from the lips of those who have neglected to lift the voice of praise and practice the grace of communion. Nevertheless, if a Christian should find himself in the position of crying out to God after having neglected him, it should move him to seek from then on to establish a life of communion and fellowship with God.

What we have been discussing is perseverance in prayer, not perseverance in *a* prayer. There are many who seem to feel that perseverance must include not only the building of a habit of prayer but the tenacious demand that God grant our particular requests. One writer has said, "God responds to the prayer of the man who refuses to take 'no' for an answer."[63] We very often hear men say something of this sort: "If one prays long enough and hard enough and believes without doubting, God will grant his request." Others have been guilty of saying, "If we persist in a petition for something that is not good for us, God may grant our request." It seems to me that such conceptions of prayer are sub-Christian, to say the least. The teachings of the New Testament do not seem to support the idea that men should lay hold of any single request or petition and "storm the gates of heaven" until it be granted.

It may be objected that the parable of the "importunate friend" (Luke 11:5–8) teaches that prayer to be successful must be "importunate and persevering."[64] Before we can come to a conclusion about the exact implications of this parable, it is necessary to look at it rather closely. The story is one that might have happened repeatedly in ancient Palestine. Since travel was often done at night to avoid the heat of the day, it would not be surprising if, on some occasions, friends arrived when there was no bread in the house to feed them and at "midnight." In such a case, what is more natural than that one should go to his

neighbor's house and ask for bread? The story implies that th
neighbor has the bread, that he is even willing to give it to h
friend, but he does not do so at once because it is inconvenie
for him. The inconvenience arises from the custom of peasa
people in Palestine of sleeping in a row on the floor of th
one-room house, one parent on each end, the children in th
middle. To arise and open the door would involve wakir
the children and disturbing the whole household. What pare
would not understand the reluctance of the friend at this ho
of the night?

However, the man who needs bread continues to knock an
ask. His plea is finally answered, not because of friendship, b
because of "importunity." The Greek word translated "impo
tunity" literally means the absence of shame. The picture th
springs to one's mind as he reads is of the importunate o
continuing to knock and pound upon the door of the hous
unashamed that he is disturbing the whole neighborhood
order to satisfy his own desires. Finally, the reluctant hous
holder arises and grants the request.

It is universally recognized by interpreters that this is a parab
by way of contrast, that there is no intention on the part
Jesus to say that God is a reluctant giver of his bounties whe
we cry out for them. God may seem thus to us, but he is n
actually so. However, there is a tendency on the part of son
interpreters to think that the action of the "importunate" o
is a true picture of the proper approach of the worshiper
prayer, that prayer must be importunate if it is to be successf
even though God be anxious to give. One interpreter says that th
meaning of the parable is: "If perseverance achieves its end
everyday human relationships, how much more in our relatio
ships with God!"[65] Another suggests: "What Jesus says is,
brief: you also will get what you want from God, as certain
as the man in my tale got what he wanted; therefore pray o
imitating his *anaideia* (i.e., shamelessness)."[66]

I must take exception to these interpretations. They seem
contradict all that we know of God and all that we are taug
about the communion of prayer. I would be inclined to agr

with the interpreter who believes that the "importunate" friend, rather than being a true example of prayer, is a warning against the use of such "importunity" in our relationship with God. The parable would thus be a discouragement of such persistence and an encouragement to ask "trustfully" rather than "importunately."[67] If this be the true import of the parable, the contrast would hold not only for the giver but for the petitioner. Jesus would then be saying, "If men, even though evil and selfish, are moved by importunity to grant your requests, how much more will God, who longs, as the all-loving Father, to help His children, hear and answer the prayers of those who in earnestness and patience pray to Him?"[68]

Perhaps the true meaning of the parable is found in remembering the opening question, "Which of you who has a friend will go to him at midnight and say to him . . . ?" The implication is that this is the natural consequence of friendship. Friends feel free to call on friends for help, and expect them to answer just because they are friends. In this case, the power of friendship had to be supplemented by persistence. Not so in the case of God. It is natural for God's children to call on him when they have need, and he never fails to answer just because he is God. He answers, not because of the persistence and importunity of the child, but because of his own love and delight in giving good things to his children. The Christian should always think of God as ready and willing to come to his aid in any circumstance of life; he should develop the habit of asking, and he will experience the blessing of continually receiving. "The parable is meant to stimulate not so much perseverance in prayer as faith that their prayers will be answered. 'If even a man with so many reasons for being disobliging,' runs the argument, 'can be moved to give what you ask, how much more will God lend a ready ear to his children's request.' "[69]

Another parable that is often used to enforce the teaching that persistence is essential to effective prayer is that of the unjust judge (Luke 18:1–8). According to Luke, the parable was meant to teach the fact that men "ought always to pray and not lose heart." The Greek word that is translated "ought" means that prayer is a necessity in the purpose of God. "Always" points to the continuity of prayer as a habit of life, literally meaning "at all times"; it is an adverb of time. "To pray" is expressed in the present infinitive, which emphasizes the continuity of practice that the other words in the application suggest. The danger that is envisioned if we do not continue the habit of prayer is that we will "lose heart." The reason for "losing heart" is not expressed here. Some have suggested that the meaning of the parable is found in the teaching that we should keep praying *"persistently* in spite of the temptation to cease praying through delayed an-swer—keep praying, notwithstanding delay. The whole *raison d'être* of the parable is the existence of such delay."[70] Others have noted that the opening introduction of the prayer is related to the previous chapter's teaching on the final advent of the Lord and that perhaps the delay is the delay in the coming of Christ. With this is connected verse eight, which says, "Nevertheless, when the Son of man comes, will he find faith on earth?"

Another possible suggestion is that "losing heart" is a danger in the face of the difficulty and persecution that accompanies service to God. Paul uses the same word to deny that he loses heart because of the blindness of Israel (II Cor. 4:1) or because of his own light affliction (v. 16). If this is the clue to our passage, it would mean that the servant of God must maintain his fellowship with God through prayer to avoid the danger of despair in the face of the adversaries of the gospel of Christ. In any case, the danger is real and the cure is prayer.

The parable itself (Luke 18:2–5) might be a common enough story in the days when justice was more often for sale than not. A widow with a worthy cause can find no satisfaction from the judge who actually and consciously regards no man and does not fear God. He is not moved by any moral principle; he acts only on his own whim. Since the widow has nothing to move him except right, he refuses her request. However, her continual coming irritates him to the extent that he grants her request to be rid of her.

The second application of this parable, either that of the Lord or that of the early Christian community, is contained in the exclamation: "And shall not God avenge his own elect, which cry day and night unto him, though he bear long with them? I tell you that he will avenge them speedily."

At least two contrasts between God and the unjust judge are expressed in these verses. One is the basis of action. The judge acts by caprice without regard for men or right; God acts from love with full concern for right and for men. The other is the speed of action. The judge delays his action until forced into it by the persistence of the widow; God acts speedily, though delay may be involved in the words "though he bear long with them."

It must be admitted that the interpretation of this parable is not as simple as that of the importunate friend; at least it does not appear to me to be so. There is more reason to suppose that the parable involves a long delay of some desired thing, perhaps the end of the world and the inauguration of the eternal Kingdom. There is more reason for supposing that the Christian is to pray for one thing, one particular thing, in spite of delay, until it is given, though God "may bear long with them." Yet, in spite of this, it would seem that the comment of Dr. Hunter is more to the point. "Need we say that Jesus is not describing some dourly ungracious Deity who requires to be badgered into compliance? As in the previous parable, the argument is 'by contraries.' If even this unprincipled judge could be moved by the widow's importunity into action, how much more will God answer his people's prayers for vindication!"[71]

What has been said does not necessarily mean that a particular request should never be repeated. There are prayers that are meant to be repeated every day; for instance: "Give us this day our daily bread," or "forgive us our debts." To pray thus each day is not really to repeat the same petition; rather, it is to repeat a similar petition under developing circumstances. It is not the bread of yesterday's need that we seek, nor the forgiveness of yesterday's sin; it is today's bread and today's sin concerning which we pray.

In some cases, however, such as the petition for the salvation of a lost friend, one might very well be led to repeat day after day the same petition for that friend. The point is that such a repetition should never involve a spirit of "importunity" as if God were not anxious to grant our request. We may be sure that any spiritual burden that we have for the lost man is created by God in our hearts; it is his prayer which we pray. The point of such repetition is that I should seek day after day to give God the use of my concern and my love for my friend in his program of redemption. I would need to commune with God about the conversion of that friend so that I could, under his leadership, place not only my concern but my abilities and myself at his disposal for the salvation of the lost man. To my way of thinking, persistence in such *a* prayer may mean the same thing as persistence in prayer.

One New Testament example of *a* prayer persisted in may be found in the statement of Paul that he and his friends prayed "earnestly night and day that we may see you face to face and supply what is lacking in your faith" (I Thess. 3:10). There seems to be no doubt here that Paul felt that there was a need for his presence in Thessalonica and that he continued to pray that the way might be opened for him to return there and meet that need. He felt no hesitancy in repeating the request "night and day" and in doing it "earnestly." However, there seems to be no insistence on his part that God must answer this prayer or abdicate his throne, no shameless disregard for the overruling providence of a loving Father in whose service he works. At most, this verse would indicate that even the greatest of Christians found it necessary to repeat the same petition. We who are lesser Christians need feel no shame that we must do likewise so long as we do it in the proper spirit, a spirit of faith and submission to the will of God. What we are saying is that there is a better way of prayer, a way that we may strive to achieve and find in it a more lasting peace and a more complete fellowship with the Father.

Not all prayers are "answered," not even for the great men of prayer, not even when they are made persistently and with great confidence that they will be answered. By this I mean that the man who prays does not always receive exactly what he asks for in the way that he asks for it. This is not an uncommon experience of life for those who make a habit of praying; for those who only pray occasionally, it may be a discouraging experience. I have heard people say: "I do not believe that God answers prayer at all. I prayed once for this or that; I prayed long; I prayed earnestly; I prayed, believing that I would receive what I asked. Yet the answer never came." A statement of this sort shows a fundamental misconception of the prayer fellowship between God and his people.

One example of an unanswered prayer is the prayer of Jesus in Gethsemane. The report of the prayer is abbreviated to the extent that it is impossible to discover with certainty the order of the petitions of Jesus. It seems likely that at first, as he faced the reality of the cross, his prayer was, "Abba, Father, all things are possible to thee; remove this cup from me" (Mark 14:36). The "cup" was the cup of suffering on the cross. This seems certain, though there are some who are not willing to admit that Jesus could have offered a petition which was not answered and interpret it to mean that Jesus was petitioning that he should not die of the agony in the Garden but should be permitted to die on the cross. This interpretation has never found credence among scholars and would not be likely to be found in a book on prayer, but it has had adherents among preachers. The usual, and the correct interpretation, I think, is that Jesus was praying with quite human feeling to be saved from dying on the cross. If so, his prayer was not answered. Why? The answer seems to lie in the fact that his request contradicted a more basic desire of his life. For God to have granted this request would have been for God to deny a deeper and more holy desire of the heart of Jesus. Jesus had often affirmed that he sought above all else to do the will of God. For him, the will of God included the cross. As Paul expressed it, Jesus "gave himself for our sins to deliver us from the present evil age, according to the will of our God and Father" (Gal. 1:4). God's will was the salvation of men, and this, according to the New Testament belief, demanded that Christ die on the cross for the sins of men. Therefore the prayer had to be denied. Of course, in the fellowship of prayer Jesus came to see this, and modified his request by saying, "Yet not what I will, but what thou wilt" (Mark 14:36). After repeating the prayer three times, Jesus came from the fellowship of prayer with his heart strengthened, ready to face the ordeal of the cross. In this instance, though the request was denied, the man was answered. From the communion of prayer came the courage to endure the cross in order to accomplish the will of God.

Jesus' request was denied because it would have contradicted a more basic desire of his life; Paul's request was denied because it would have kept him from experiencing a better blessing. The record of Paul's unanswered prayer is found in II Cor. 12:6–10. Paul had a "thorn . . . in the flesh" that he interpreted to be a "messenger of Satan" sent "to harass" him. To his mind, this was an unbearable burden and a hindrance in his work of preaching the gospel of Christ. Just what the thorn was, no one knows for sure. When the total evidence is considered, it seems likely that it was an affliction which caused him to be repulsive to the eyes of men in some physical way. Could one blame him for wishing to be rid of it? With desire burning in his heart, he turned to the Lord in prayer. Not once but "three times I besought the Lord about this," he says. Behind this simple sentence stands what is probably an extended period of prayer on three different occasions about this problem. There was no doubt what Paul wanted; he wanted the thorn removed. In all likelihood, his motives were pure; he was not thinking so much of personal suffering as of the hindrance to his ministry.

Again the prayer was unanswered, but the man was not. In the communion of prayer, Paul came to see that God's view of his affliction was different from his. The affliction might be a "messenger of Satan," but it was also a servant of God. God used it to keep humble a man to whom so many wonderful things had happened that pride was a real danger in his life. He said to Paul, "My grace is sufficient for you, for my power is made perfect in weakness." From this experience of prayer Paul came to realize that his affliction was essential for his own spiritual life, that it did not really interfere with his spiritual power, and said, "For the sake of Christ, then, I am content with weaknesses, insults, hardships, persecutions, and calamities; for when I am weak, then I am strong."

The answer to the problem of unanswered prayer seems, then, to lie in two directions. First, some of our requests are often contradictory to our own highest desires. That is, if they were granted, it would be impossible to grant something else that we desire more and that is in the will of God for our life. Second, some of our requests are for inferior blessings. These God denies in order that he may give us superior blessings. For instance, as a young preacher, I prayed earnestly that God might open the way for me to get an education. I conceived of this as meaning that God would move upon the heart of some man of wealth to provide the money so that I could go to school without financial worry. For two years, I kept praying for this and looking for the answer. Finally, in a period of communion with God, I came to see that my prayer was wrong. I felt it to be God's will that I go to school. Therefore I should go in my poverty and trust God to provide my needs along the way. I changed my prayer, matriculated in a college, and God saw me through nine years of study. As I look back now upon these years, I rejoice that my original prayer went unanswered. My experience was so much richer and more meaningful as I learned the lesson of daily trust for the necessities of life than it would have been if I could have lived without the necessity of depending on God for these things.

"Adoniram Judson, Massachusetts-born missionary of the last century, prayed to be sent to India, but he was compelled by circumstances to go to Burma. He prayed for his wife's life, but buried her and their two children. He prayed for release from a Burma prison, but was kept there eleven terrible months, chained and miserable.

"The missionary's petitions were not answered, but God answered the man. Judson rendered immeasurable service to the Kingdom of God in Burma, and his Burmese-English dictionary is a monument to fine scholarship. This is what Judson wrote on the subject of prayer: 'I never prayed sincerely and earnestly for anything but it came . . . no matter at how distant a day. Somehow, in some shape—probably the last that I should have devised—it came.' How wonderfully the man was answered!"[72]

Unanswered prayer should never be a discouragement to praying. If our petitions are not granted, it means that they should not be granted. As we continue to commune with God about the problem, the time will come when we can see with the perspective of God and bring our petitions into line with his will for our lives. If we were perfect in our relationship with God, if we never let human and earthly desires interfere with our perception of the will of God, perhaps we would never have the experience of an ungranted request. But this is not true of us. We must reckon with our imperfections and our sinful desires even in our prayer life. The result of unanswered petitions in prayer should be that we develop the habit of constant prayer and communion with God, that we present our requests to God, but never with an adamant insistence that they be granted in just the form we ask. Such "persistence in *a* prayer" could very well blind us to the higher purposes of God without even accomplishing the granting of the thing we ask.

What of delay in the answer to our prayers? God's time to give does not always coincide with our time to ask. Some people have supposed that God deliberately delays to answer some of our petitions for the good of the worshiper. One writer has suggested that delay "is in order to develop faith, since it is tenacity in prayer in the face of disappointment that deepens faith."[73] Another writer agrees with this reason but gives others as well, among which is the supposition that delay of the answer will purify the motives of the worshiper so that what he asks will now be asked, after delay, for the right motive. He also suggests that delay may be for the reason of deepening and intensifying our desires.[74] There may be truth in these suggestions. It is certainly true that if prayer were a sort of Aladdin's lamp that yielded instant results at our slightest whim, it would become a weapon of destruction.[75] However, it seems to me that these suggestions miss the point of the New Testament teaching on prayer. No prayer is meaningful unless it is prayed in the proper spirit. Delay in receiving what we ask for in the wrong spirit is not delay but refusal. Even though the thing we ask for may happen, it cannot be said to be the result of our prayer, unless we pray in faith. Nor is it possible to think of prayer as a means of granting our slightest whim; prayer is a means of bringing God's will to pass.

What we are thinking about here is a petition that we make in the proper spirit, a proper petition, one that God intends to grant in his own time, the best time, but the answer is delayed. How should this affect our prayer life? Should we continue to cry out unto God to grant our request, or is there a better and more Christian solution to our problem? Is this a time when persistence in *a* prayer is justified and proper? It would seem that this is not the case. The problem is not so much in the delay of the answer, but in our ability to perceive the answer. We may learn the proper spirit here from the words of Jesus: "Therefore I tell you, whatever you ask in prayer, believe that you receive it, and you will" (Mark 11:24). The Greek tense behind this verse would better be rendered, in the central portion, "believe that you did receive (or have received) it." The picture that is presented by this verse is that of the petitioner praying and coming to believe, even while he is praying, that his prayer has been answered, that he has received his request. He may look up and find that in actuality he has not received it; it may be days, months, even years before the actual fulfillment of the request takes place. Yet he has "received it." He has come to know within his heart that God has granted his request and he is able to follow the advice of the old song: "Take your burdens to the Lord and leave them there." Perhaps an earthly illustration will help us here. Suppose I should ask a friend to contribute his money to help me in some enterprise of the future. Suppose, further, that my friend promises that he will give me a hundred dollars toward this enterprise when the need actually arises but does not in fact put the money in my hands at the time. Has my request been granted? Yes. Has the answer been delayed? Yes. However, in spite of the fact that I do not actually have the money, I continue to plan and act as if I actually did have it. I believe my friend; he has promised—his promise is as good as the money. It would be an insult to my friend for me to return the following day or week and demand that he renew his promise. When the time comes, he will fulfill his promise; until then, I wait with confidence.

What I am suggesting is that our prayer communion with God can be and should be of this nature. The belief that we have received is, of course, not an achievement of our mind; it is a conviction resting on the impartation to our spirit of the confidence that God has granted our request. One could, of course, be misled at this point by superficiality in prayer; he might work himself up to believe that God has granted what he has not actually granted. There is a danger that we may take too much for granted. However, the fact remains that God has the power to impart such assurance to our spirits, and that he actually does so on occasion. That he does not do so on others is not due to his reluctance, but to our inability to perceive. The possibility is there; the ideal is that for which we should strive in our communion with God.

What should be our reaction in the face of uncertainty that arises from our inability to perceive? Perhaps the answer here would lie not so much in repeating the request as such; once we are sure of what we should ask, once we are convinced that this is in the will of God, once we have presented our petition in faith, we should leave it to God to answer in his own good time. However, God knows our frame; he understands our weakness. Perhaps we may now return the next day or the next week when the answer is delayed in fact and say: "Lord, I asked for this; I believe it is right that you should give it. Yet I do not have the assurance in my heart that you will. Will you now give me that assurance so that I may leave the matter in your hands and turn my energies in other directions that are within your will." Such a prayer as this would surely be proper and would lead to the assurance and peace we seek.

Some have suggested that in such circumstances, we should "put out the fleece" after the example of Gideon. This is the Biblical way, we are told, to discover and make sure of the will of God in our lives. Some persons have supposed that God directed them to go to school by having the hens lay so many eggs on a given day; some ministers have supposed that God was directing them to resign a pastorate because a certain number of people, which they had asked to be saved as a "sign" from God, were not saved. The trouble with this suggestion is twofold. One problem is to discover a proper test. If we choose something that might happen without the interference of God, we leave ourselves open to spiritual direction from unspiritual sources. If we choose something that demands the action of God, we may be in the position of asking God to do something as a "sign" that he would do anyway if it were possible. At best, we are engaging in a sub-Christian practice. We are selling our Christian birthright for a mess of pottage that consists of outward signs. The Christian has the right and privilege of direct communion with God; he should exercise that right rather than forfeit it.

I tried this once. When I was wrestling with my call to the ministry, I asked God to give a conversion at a service in which I was to speak, if he really wanted me to be a preacher. The service came and even as I spoke all doubts dissolved and I knew that this was God's call to me. A young lady was converted. Others came and assured me that they believed I had been called by God to preach. This was like frosting on the cake, but the reality was that God had convinced me of his will by direct communion. Through thirty years in the ministry, I have never doubted my call to the ministry, and this not because the "sign" I asked for actually happened—it was, in my inner consciousness, an anticlimax—but because God communicated directly to me his will for my life.

There is still another subject that we must consider when we think of persistence in prayer, the subject of struggle in prayer. There is a popular conception of prayer which says that the only way to success in prayer is through struggle, through agonizing, through "paying the price."[76] Although those who speak thus are usually not clear about the meaning of what they say, it would seem that the implication of "agonizing in prayer" is that this is the way God is persuaded to grant our requests. Can this be true? We have already noted that God needs no persuasion to grant good things to his children and that no amount of persuasion could cause him to give bad things. How, then, can "agonizing in prayer" be thought of as a necessary exercise on the part of the Christian in order to gain the answer to our prayers?

But some will object that we have Biblical examples of men who did struggle with God in order to gain his blessings. One of the most popular examples is that of Jacob's supposed wrestling with the Lord (Gen. 32:22–32). Aside from the fact that Old Testament examples of prayer are often sub-Christian, the story does not say that Jacob wrestled with the Lord, but that "a man wrestled with him [i.e., Jacob] until the breaking of the day" (v. 24). The point of the passage seems to be that the Lord wrestled with Jacob to bring him to a consciousness of his need rather than that Jacob wrestled with the Lord to gain the blessing. When Jacob finally asked for the blessing, he received it without delay in the form of a new name which indicated his new role in redemptive history. There are, however, New Testament examples of a certain relationship between "agonizing" and prayer. One is the prayer of Jesus in Gethsemane: "And being in an agony he prayed more earnestly; and his sweat became like great drops of blood falling down upon the ground" (Luke 22:44). Another is the example of Epaphras, who, according to Paul, was "always striving for" [Greek, "agonizing for"] the Colossians in his prayers in order that they might "stand fast in all the will of God" (Col. 4:12, my translation). The final example is that of Paul. He says to the Colossians, "I want you to know how greatly I strive [Greek, "agonize"] for you, and for those at Laodicea, and for all who have not seen my face" (Col. 2:1). Though prayer is not explicitly related to "agonizing" in this verse, it would seem likely that prayer is what Paul had in mind.

The Greek word *agōn,* which lies behind these references, was used, in the ordinary language of the first century, of fighting in a war or competing in a race or participating in a wrestling match. It has passed over into the English language as our word "agony," which primarily expresses the idea of great pain. We must remember that, in the New Testament, the idea of pain is never primarily involved. The primary idea is that of struggle or conflict.

But with whom do we struggle in the conflict of prayer? Surely not with God. As this word stands in connection with prayer it implies that one's desires are opposed by spiritual enemies and victory depends on deep earnestness of prayer. Who are these spiritual enemies? The answer seems to be that they are the carnal and selfish desires that seek to dominate our own life, promoted, no doubt, by the ministry of Satan. The struggle, if this is the case, is not with God but with ourselves, or at least with Satan as he manifests himself in our lives. This concept fits perfectly into the New Testament examples where prayer and struggle are related. As we have already noted, Jesus had to struggle with his own quite human desire to avoid the suffering of the cross before he could come to pray with deep sincerity, "Thy will be done." Paul, no doubt, had to struggle with his preoccupation with the needs of those around him before he found sincere concern for the affairs of those whom he had never seen. Epaphras, likewise, must have struggled with his preoccupation with his own position before he could sincerely intercede for the absent brothers in Colossae. No implication exists in any of these stories of a reluctant God who must be moved by the agony and struggle of the worshiper before he will grant the request.

A fitting conclusion to this section, which suggests that continuous prayer, habitual prayer, is the only effective prayer, is found in Paul's admonition to the Philippian church. "Stop worrying about anything. The cure of worry is to turn to God in every experience of life, making known to him your requests in the spirit of prayer and supplication, not forgetting to be thankful for his past blessings and continued help. If you do this, the peace that comes from God and surpasses any sense of security based on earthly circumstances shall guard your hearts and minds in your union with Christ." (Phil. 4:6–7, my paraphrase.) Prayer for the Christian, then, should become a way of life; all of life should be saturated in the spirit of prayer. It might well be said that no Christian life is what it should be until it has become a life of effective, dynamic, powerful prayer.

Church and Prayer—Synopsis

Jesus intended that his churches should be prayer fellowships, and left instruction to that end.

If the church is to pronounce the sentence of heaven on the actions of men, it must seek leadership through prayer.

The first church took seriously its role as a prayer fellowship. The book of The Acts records many instances of prayer by church fellowships.

Power was received through prayer for the witnessing mission of the church.

Guidance was received through prayer in the selection of leadership for the church.

Boldness to continue witnessing in spite of threats by Jewish rulers was found through prayer.

The great doctrinal controversy of the first century found its solution through the practice of prayer.

The foreign mission movement of the first century received its impulse in a prayer meeting.

In these passages, a pattern is set for the modern church in fulfilling its stewardship as a body of Christ.

X

The Church and Prayer

Jesus intended that his churches should be prayer fellowships and he gave instructions to this end. Most of the passages that we have studied apply equally to the church fellowship and to the private devotions of the individual Christian. The same principles of prayer would prevail in corporate as well as in individual prayer.

However, the subject is of such importance that it is worthwhile to study the passages that clearly relate themselves to the idea of the church fellowship. In the recorded teachings of Jesus, one passage is of particular significance—Matt. 18:15–20. There is no need to assume that these verses "are not a transcript of his very words, but a reflection of the thought and practice of the early church."[77] The tendency to discount Matthew's record of the instructions of Jesus to his disciples concerning their life as a church is based upon an imagined "hierarchical tendency" in Matthew. I would agree with Filson, who says that to find a rigid church organization in Matthew is to "play fast and loose with the evidence."[78] He insists that "nothing justifies the view that Jesus could not have spoken these words."[79]

In the passage, four actions of the church are anticipated: the exercise of discipline (v. 17), the exercise of the authority of heaven in binding and loosing (v. 18), praying (v. 19), and gathering in the name of Jesus (v. 20). These actions are vitally related. Our understanding of the teaching of Jesus about prayer will depend on our understanding of what is meant by the other verses in the passage. First, the church is commanded to exercise discipline over its members, even if it must excommunicate a recalcitrant sinner. The situation that is envisioned by the paragraph is that in which one member of the church "sins" against another brother. This becomes a serious matter, since the fellowship of the church is then disturbed and the ability of the church to act as a body of Christ is destroyed. Such a condition must not be ignored. Every effort is to be made to gain the brother back to the Christian fellowship. The wronged brother is to seek reconciliation. Only when he fails is he to bring other Christians into partnership with him in his effort to restore fellowship. If they fail, the matter must be brought to the church. If the recalcitrant one "refuses to listen even to the church, let him be to you as a Gentile and a tax collector" (v. 17).

Such action is not to be taken flippantly; it must be a responsible exercise on the part of the church of its position as the body of Jesus Christ. This, I think, is the import of the saying: "Truly, I say to you, whatever you bind on earth shall be bound in heaven, and whatever you loose on earth shall be loosed in heaven" (v. 18). What is meant by this difficult verse? The key to its interpretation is found in the verb tenses, which are almost universally obscured in English translations (cf. Matt. 16:19; John 20:23). The RSV translation, quoted above, makes the verb tense a simple future: "Whatever you bind . . . shall be bound" and "whatever you loose . . . shall be loosed." This translation has led commentators to say that the teaching of Jesus is that the action of the church will be "ratified in heaven, i.e., by God."[80] This misses the fact that the verb tenses in the Greek are the future perfect, not the simple future. They should be rendered thus: "What you bind . . . will have been bound" and "what you loose . . . will have been loosed." Or, as one translator has put it: "Whatever you forbid on earth must be already forbidden in heaven, and whatever you permit on earth must be already permitted in heaven."[81]

The importance of this distinction of tenses is great because it reveals the role of the church as the representative spokesman for heaven. (Note: there can be no doubt that the church is the agency that binds and looses on earth; the context as well as the plural pronoun make this plain.) The prior binding and loosing takes place in heaven; the earthly binding and loosing only pronounces the sentence of heaven. We do not have heaven ratifying or sanctioning what the church has done (the usual interpretation). We have the church announcing what heaven has done.

This is an awesome responsibility; the disciple band stood confronted with the necessity of pronouncing the sentence of heaven on the actions of men. How were they to know the sentence of heaven? The answer is revealed in the following verses; it lies in the practice of corporate, Spirit-led prayer. For clarity of discussion, let us reverse the order of the verses. The second contains the promise: "Where two or three are gathered in my name, there am I in the midst of them" (Matt. 18:20). The "two or three" gathered in the name of Jesus is the church in its simplest expression. The two or three may become thousands, but the thing that constitutes them as a church is still the same. They must be gathered together in Jesus' name. We have discussed the meaning of this term above and need only remind ourselves that it means "as Jesus' representatives." A body of people, even a body of Christians, is not a church unless it is assembled to do business in the name of Jesus. But if it is so assembled, be it large or small in number, the group becomes a church of Jesus Christ. Our verse tells us that there is an unseen presence in such a group. Jesus is there in their midst.

Now the church prays. The object of prayer is not specified, but the context would indicate that it is for the guidance of heaven in the treatment of the sinful brother. Perhaps at the beginning of the prayer, the minds of the various members are not in harmony. Their prayer cannot be answered. But in the act of prayer something happens; agreement comes; their prayer is answered. Jesus promised, "If two of you agree on earth about anything they ask, it will be done for them by my Father in heaven" (v. 19). This does not mean that two men may discuss between themselves what they shall ask of God, agree on their petition, and thus be assured of its answer. The verse has often been wrested from its context and made a program for forcing God to conform to the desire of men. The picture becomes clear in its context. It is the church at prayer. The members agree. "The Greek word *symphōneō* is used primarily of musical instruments that make the same sound."[82] This presents a beautiful picture of the church speaking the same petition.

But how does this agreement come? I think the context makes it clear that it comes through the unseen presence of Jesus. It is his Spirit moving upon theirs that leads them to see and understand the will of heaven and pray unitedly for it to be done. Once they have come to agreement on these terms, the members of the church, acting as one, may fulfill their responsibility as spokesman of heaven. What they "bind or loose" will now be what has already been "bound or loosed" in heaven.

If my interpretation of this passage is correct, the passage reveals what should be the principle of church action always. The church (any church) should consider itself a representative of Christ, acting in his name. It should be willing to assume its role in history, not proudly or boastfully, but humbly. To ensure the faithful performance of its stewardship, it must become a prayer fellowship. Sincere and earnest prayer must be a part of its assembling. Only as the church is moved by the Holy Spirit to symphonize its petitions can it be sure that heaven has answered. Only in this way can a church be assured that it is really a church of the Lord Jesus Christ.

The first church took Jesus at his word; it became a fellowship of prayer. Prayer became a vital and dynamic element in the corporate life of the church. First, we notice that they received power for the fulfillment of their mission through prayer. The mission that they had been assigned was a staggering one. They were only 120 strong, and Jesus had said to them, "You shall be my witnesses in Jerusalem and in all Judea and Samaria and to the end of the earth" (Acts 1:8). Where was this small band of disciples to receive power for such a task? The answer for them lay where it must lie for every church of Jesus Christ in any age as it faces any task. The power must come from God. With the commission, a promise was given: "You shall receive power when the Holy Spirit has come upon you" (v. 8a). The program for the reception of power had been laid down by Jesus in his words: "Behold, I send the promise of my Father upon you; but stay in the city, until you are clothed with power from on high" (Luke 24:49). Two notations are made of the prayers of the church. "They returned to Jerusalem with great joy, and were continually in the temple blessing God." (Vs. 52-53.) "All these with one accord devoted themselves to prayer, together with the women and Mary the mother of Jesus, and with his brothers." (Acts 1:14.) Between the ascension of Jesus and Pentecost, the church spent ten days in prayer. The result is an open book for all to read. "When the day of Pentecost had come, they were all together in one place. And suddenly a sound came from heaven like the rush of a mighty wind. . . . And they were all filled with the Holy Spirit and began to speak in other tongues, as the Spirit gave them utterance." (Acts 2:1-4.) "And there were added that day about three thousand souls." (V. 41.)

What a revival! It came when the power of God came on a praying church. Many of our modern churches with their numerous members, fine buildings, and full programs do not win three thousand souls to Christ in a generation, let alone in one day. Why? The answer may lie in the fact that we are not, like the first church, endued with the power of the Holy Spirit. And perhaps the reason for that is that our modern churches are not true prayer fellowships. If we prayed, God could give us the power we need for our task. Perhaps it would not be another Pentecost, but the rivers of blessings would be of the same nature.

Secondly, we notice that the first church received guidance in selecting its leaders through prayer. The clearest record of this type of leadership through prayer is found in the selection of a successor to Judas (Acts 1:15-26). Remember, the church was engaged in a continual prayer meeting for the coming of the power of God. While they prayed, Peter interrupted the prayer meeting to call a business meeting of the church. No doubt acting under the impulsion of divine guidance, he suggested that a qualified witness should be chosen to fill out the number of the Twelve. He enumerated the qualifications the new apostle should have, saying: "One of the men who have accompanied us during all the time that the Lord Jesus went in and out among us, beginning from the baptism of John until the day when he was taken up from us—one of these men must become with us a witness to his resurrection" (vs. 21–22). The church members, acting democratically, "put forward two," i.e., they nominated two men for the office. In most of our churches such a situation would call for speeches and a voting contest to see which man would be chosen. Not so with this church. Having expressed their mind and finding that they were not in agreement, they sought the guidance of God. They prayed and said, "Lord, who knowest the hearts of all men, show which one of these two thou hast chosen" (v. 24).

Having prayed, they "cast lots for them" (v. 26). This is the only place in the New Testament where this interesting practice is mentioned. In Old Testament times, casting lots was a common way of finding the will of God. After the coming of the Holy Spirit, it seems to have vanished from the life of the church. Perhaps the reason is that the direct guidance of the Holy Spirit is the birthright of a church of Jesus Christ. Such external means of discerning the will of God as "casting lots" or "putting out the fleece" belong to the infancy of true religion, not to its maturity. At any rate, on this occasion, they cast lots and "the lot fell on Matthias."

The church considered this to be a revelation of God's choice, and "he was enrolled with the eleven apostles" (v. 26). The Greek word that is translated "enrolled" (*sugkatapsēphizomai*) really means "to be chosen by a vote." It is found in only one other place in Greek literature, where seven men are said to have joined in a vote of condemnation.[83] I think the evidence is sufficient to justify us in supposing that after the casting of lots, a poll of the church was taken. It was unanimous for God's choice of Matthias.

Do you suppose that this might suggest a way for modern churches to conduct their business? If a church exists to carry out the will of God in all its actions, should not prayer be a vital part of all its decisions? Often our church business meetings become debating societies or political campaigns rather than praying fellowships. It would seem to me that the practice of dynamic prayer would solve the difficulties of our human disagreements.

This seems to have been the case also in the selection of the seven (Acts 6:1–7). Murmuring arose in the congregation, now numbering more than five thousand male members (Acts 4:4). The bone of contention was the feeding of the widows. One group, the Hellenists (Jewish Christians whose home was in the Greek world), felt that their widows were being neglected. Though it is not specified, it is almost certain that the Twelve, if not the whole church, made this a matter of prayer. The solution that the Twelve proposed was to choose seven members of the church to see to this matter, while the Twelve would devote themselves "to prayer and to the ministry of the word" (Acts 6:4). This pleased the congregation; seven men were selected. Hebrews (Jewish Christians whose home was in Palestine) joined with the Hellenists in electing seven Hellenists to oversee this matter. What a demonstration of the spirit of love! It is not likely that this was done without prayer. When the selection was made, the apostles "prayed and laid their hands upon them. And the word of God increased; and the number of the disciples multiplied greatly in Jerusalem, and a great many of the priests were obedient to the faith" (vs. 6–7). The problem of internal dissension had been solved in the atmosphere of prayer; this is how it should always be.

Again, the first church found courage to persevere in their witnessing through prayer. The first days of the church were stormy ones. After Peter and John had healed the lame man, they were arrested for preaching the resurrection. At their defense, no opportunity was found for condemnation by the rulers of the Jews, but a warning was issued against their continued preaching. "So they called them and charged them not to speak or teach at all in the name of Jesus." (Acts 4:18.) This was no idle charge; these were the same rulers that had contrived the death of Jesus. "When they were released they went to their friends and reported what the chief priests and the elders had said to them." (V. 23.) What now shall the church do? What would a modern church do under like circumstances? This church prayed. "They lifted their voices together to God." (V. 24.) What did they pray for? What would we pray for? The essence of their request was: "And now, Lord, look upon their threats, and grant to thy servants to speak thy word with all boldness" (v. 29). No petition for protection or safety. No petition for wisdom to speak in private. Just a petition for "boldness" to continue to speak in spite of the threats of the rulers. Their prayer was answered. "When they had prayed, the place in which they were gathered together was shaken; and they were all filled with the Holy Spirit and spoke the word of God with boldness." (V. 31.) This church overcame its fears by prayer.

A final note of prayer by the first church, though other churches were now involved, occurred during the great doctrinal controversy of the early years of Christianity. Perhaps the incident would suggest the way by which modern Christians might settle their theological and denominational differences. The point of controversy was the circumcision of Gentile converts. Was it essential to salvation and to church fellowship? Some of the Christians felt that it was. They believed that God's promises were to the Jews alone; the coming of Christ had not changed that. Therefore, faith in Christ was only the first step in salvation for the Gentiles, though it was sufficient for salvation for the Jews. Gentiles must also be circumcised and become proselyte Jews.

Other Christians saw it differently. They believed that faith in Christ brought salvation to all men. The promises of God had been to the Jewish nation, but the coming of Christ had changed that. The promise was now unto all men. Stephen had been put to death for preaching this. Paul took up the light and carried it on in his missionary journeys. The experience of Peter with Cornelius seems to have been thought of as an exceptional case; perhaps Cornelius was accepted as a "devout man." The Judaizing party (this became their name) went to Antioch and demanded that Gentiles be circumcised. Paul objected. A conference was held in Jerusalem to settle the difficulty. (Acts, ch. 15; cf. Gal. 2:1–10.)

Much debate occurred. The opposing parties were adamant in their positions. Finally, a decision was made, perhaps the most important theological decision of the ages. It was that salvation was for all men, on the simple condition of faith. Our concern here is how that decision was reached. Was it a result of compromise? No. One side won a clear-cut decision. It is not always true that there are three sides to a debate—your side, my side, and the right side. Christian people must learn to admit that they could be wrong; they must learn to seek God's side of the debate. Only then can Christian unity become a living and lasting reality.

Was the decision reached through good theological thinking? This certainly played a part in it. Both accounts of the conference record instances of good theological thought, thought that was divorced from selfish ends. But this alone would never have solved the difficulty. It never does. Theological debate does not create a climate for surrender; it usually ends in both sides maintaining their own position.

I think the decision was ultimately reached through prayer. This is indicated in the letter that James wrote and sent out to the Christian world in the name of the Jerusalem church. The key clause, which reveals that the decision was wrought in prayer, is, "For it has seemed good to the Holy Spirit and to us" (Acts 15:28). This could not have been said unless the church in prayer had come to know what the mind of the Holy Spirit was. All other resources were used: debate, argument, testimony; the ultimate decision rested on prayer.

Wouldn't it be possible for the modern Christian world to act in the same way? Couldn't we decide to submit our differences to the judgment of God? Compromise is not the answer.

Denominational pride is not the answer. Theological debate is not the answer. We have tried all of these. It would seem that the only way modern Christianity can ever speak with one voice is to let that voice be the voice of God. If this is ever to happen, it will have to happen through the practice of prayer.

Let us consider one more note on the church and prayer in the book of The Acts. The Christian missionary movement arose out of a prayer meeting. It is well known that most missionary movements have arisen in this way. The "Haystack prayer meeting" is the well-known source of the modern foreign mission movement in America. The first missionary movement arose in Antioch. The record tells us that five "prophets and teachers" were "worshiping the Lord and fasting" as the Holy Spirit spoke to them (Acts 13:1–2). His command to the church, through its leaders, was that Paul and Barnabas, the two most gifted men, were to be set apart "for the work to which" he had "called them." The church obeyed; the impulse received through prayer was not quenched. "Then after fasting and praying they laid their hands on them and sent them off." (V. 3.) Missions, then as now, rides on the "wings of prayer."

Prayer was a vital and dynamic part of the life of the churches in the first century. After Pentecost, it is said that the church devoted itself to four things: the apostles' teaching, fellowship, breaking of bread, and prayers (Acts 2:42). The continuing life of the church is described. "And day by day, attending the temple together and breaking bread in their homes, they partook of food with glad and generous hearts, praising God and having favor with all the people." (Vs. 46–47.) Prayer was a part of the process of appointing elders in "every church" that had been founded by Paul on the first missionary journey (Acts 14:23). Prayer occurred at leave-taking (Acts 20:36) from the elders of Ephesus and from the disciples at Tyre (Acts 21:5). Prayer was the order of the day when Paul met the escort of Christians at Three Taverns (Acts 28:15). Thanksgiving was part of the common worship of the churches (Eph. 5:17–20). Harmony was to be sought, that together they might "with one voice glorify the God and Father" of the Lord Jesus Christ (Rom. 15:6).

But enough has been said to show that the New Testament teaches that prayer is a necessity in a church of the Lord Jesus Christ. In prayer, power may be found to witness; leaders may be chosen wisely through prayer; internal dissension may be overcome through prayer; boldness may be received through prayer; theological controversy may be settled in prayer; the missionary spirit is fanned to a blaze through prayer. Prayer is our birthright as churches of Christ; we must pray or we will become mere societies of men.

Service and Prayer—Synopsis

Service and prayer are twin virtues that must not be separated in the Christian life.

The essential relation of service to prayer and prayer to service is indicated in the teachings of Jesus and the experiences of early Christians as recorded in the book of The Acts.

The Christian view of service, which teaches that God works through us, would necessarily mean that service could be rendered only through a man of prayer.

It is through prayer that Christians are inspired to serve and encouraged amid the discouragements of service.

Through prayer, the Christian servant receives the guidance of the Holy Spirit.

Through prayer, the Christian servant receives the attending power of God.

XI

Service and Prayer

What we have already said indicates that service and prayer are twin Christian virtues. Service without the practice of prayer is powerless; prayer that does not anticipate service is pagan. These virtues are Siamese twins that cannot be separated without the certainty that both will die.

The vital connection between service and prayer is made clear in the words of Jesus to his disciples on the crucifixion eve. Jesus reminded his disciples that he had chosen them for the purpose of service: "You did not choose me, but I chose you and appointed you that you should go and bear fruit and that your fruit should abide; so that whatever you ask the Father in my name, he may give it to you" (John 15:16). The English translation tends to obscure the syntax of this verse. There are two purpose clauses connected with the verbs "chose" and "appointed." The first clause states that the purpose which he had in choosing and appointing them was that they might bear fruit, i.e., render service in his Kingdom. The second clause states that the purpose he had in choosing and appointing them was that they might ask the Father in the name of Jesus and receive that for which they asked, i.e., that they might pray effectively. The context indicates that these two purposes are really one; they are the reverse sides of the same coin. The disciples' lot in life is service and prayer: prayer in order to have power in service; service that is inspired and endured through prayer.

The same connection between prayer and service is indicated in another passage: "He who believes in me will also do the works that I do; and greater works than these will he do, because I go to the Father. Whatever you ask in my name, I will do it, that the Father may be glorified in the Son; if you ask anything in my name, I will do it" (John 14:12–14). Notice the straight line of development from the promise of unlimited power in service to the promise of unlimited resources through prayer. Though it is not specifically stated that power will be given only to those who intend to use it in service, it is implied that this is true. Though it is not specifically said that the mighty works which believers shall do depend on the power that they receive through the practice of prayer, this is plainly the implication of the verses.

The experience of those who seek to pray gives validity to this essential connection. When we pray with selfishness, "to spend it on . . . [our] passions" (James 4:3), we receive nothing from God. However, when we throw our whole being into the service of God, when we are concerned about living "in the name of Christ," we find the way open to ask anything of God, and we see his bountiful answers on every hand.

The early church recognized that prayer was an essential element in the ministry of the apostles (Acts 6:4) and elected the seven to free their hands from the service of tables that they might devote themselves to the practice of prayer. Paul did not hesitate to request God to give him a safe and prosperous journey to Rome in order that he might impart a spiritual gift to the Roman Christians (Rom. 1:10–11). Nor did he think it unseemly to pray "earnestly night and day" that he might see the Thessalonian Christians face to face and supply what was lacking in their faith (I Thess. 3:10). We see then that the early Christians thought of prayer as a resource that was essential to their service of God. They believed that service without prayer would be powerless and prayer without service would be an empty repetition of words.

This is, of course, to be expected when we think of the New Testament conception of the nature of service and the purpose of prayer. Service is never thought of in the New Testament as something that we do for God but as something that God does through us. The personal, mystical union between God and his servants stands constantly in the forefront. The conception of service is strange to the ears of some moderns, and even the finest Christians sometimes are inclined to think of service as something that we do for an absentee God.

We are inclined to think of service as a task, sometimes as a task to which we are called, but nevertheless a task that is primarily our responsibility. We are to apply our talents and abilities to the doing of the task with the hope that we shall accomplish good for God through it, usually with the added thought that we may win the approval and blessing of God as a result of a job well done. It is to be suspected that we think of the reward for service in terms of some result that is not itself connected with the service. For instance, we might think of being given good health because we are faithful to God or of receiving some material reward as a result of spiritual service. The whole relationship is all too often thought of in mechanical, or at the best, semipersonal, terms. Sometimes we even think of our service as service to mankind, and there are those who advise young people to enter the ministry because it is the best possible way to bring humanity good and lasting benefits.

All of this, insofar as it represents modern man's conception of service, is contrary to the New Testament.

To illustrate the New Testament conception of service, let us notice the experience of Paul, not because it is out of the norm but because we have more information from him than from others. First of all, Paul thought of his salvation as essentially related to a divine purpose for him to serve. "But when he who had set me apart before I was born, and had called me through his grace, was pleased to reveal his Son to me, in order that I might preach him among the Gentiles, I did not confer with flesh and blood." (Gal. 1:15–16.) There was no thought in the mind of Paul, nor any basis in the New Testament, for the thought in any other mind that salvation can ever be a reality without a corresponding responsibility for service to God.

Secondly, we notice that Paul looked on his service, his particular task, as a commission from God. He said: "For if I preach the gospel, that gives me no ground for boasting. For necessity is laid upon me. Woe to me if I do not preach the gospel! For if I do this of my own will, I have a reward; but if not of my own will, I am entrusted with a commission" (I Cor. 9:16–17). The words of this statement have been subject to various translations and interpretations, but it seems most likely that "If I do this of my own will" means "If I do it by my own human choice." The course of the meaning would be somewhat like this: "If I do this, that is, if I preach the gospel because I choose to, this would make it a business matter and I would be doing it because I expected a reward from my service." This is assumed to be contrary to fact. "But if I preach the gospel, not by my own choice, but by the appointment of Jesus Christ, I preach as a steward of Christ."

Thirdly, Paul thought of his service as something that gained its success through the indwelling presence of God in his life and the continued activity of God in his acts. "By the grace of God I am what I am, and his grace toward me was not in vain. On the contrary, I worked harder than any of them, though it was not I, but the grace of God which is with me." (I Cor. 15:10.) Some of the expressions in this verse need clarification. The expression "worked harder" probably refers more to the results of the labor rather than to the difficulty or constancy of it. The Greek is literally "more abundantly" and would be more adapted to the thought of results than to working hard. The expression "the grace of God which is with me" carries with it the idea of an attending power that made the service of Paul effective. The idea that the success of service gains its reality by the presence of God is strengthened in Paul's further statements of his service as he likens his work to planting, but asserts that it is God who gives the increase (I Cor. 3:7). He even explained the plainness of his speech by saying that it was a deliberate effort on his part to avoid any suggestion that human faith was aroused by human skill in order that the faith of his listeners "might not rest in the wisdom of men but in the power of God" (I Cor. 2:5).

One more step is required if we are to understand Paul's conception of the relation of his service to the power of God; he thought of his service as being really the service of God through him. He said to the Corinthians, "So we are ambassadors for Christ, God making his appeal through us" (II Cor. 5:20). The thought that is involved in this statement goes beyond the thought of an attending power of God; it envisions the servant as being caught up in the hands of God and used as an instrument of service. It is this thought of service that catches up in it the highest and holiest conception of human companionship with God in the act of service. This is the conception that underlies Paul's important statement about the true meaning of Christian worship: "I appeal to you therefore, brethren, by the mercies of God, to present your bodies as a living sacrifice, holy and acceptable to God, which is your spiritual worship" (Rom. 12:1).

It is easy to see, when service is so conceived, how essential to effective service is the practice of prayer. Add to this the New Testament teaching that the purpose of prayer is to get God's will done in and through us, and one sees immediately that service is an essential outgrowth of prayer communion.

However, we need not rely upon the conclusions of reason, important as they are to the understanding of our subject; we have many indications in the New Testament itself of the essential relationship between service and prayer.

Let us notice some of the important results in service that come through the practice of prayer. The first of these is inspiration and encouragement of the man of God to take his place of service in the reign of God. Many commentators have noted the relationship between the command of Jesus to look on the fields that were white to harvest, to pray for the Lord of the harvest to send forth laborers into the field, and his command for the disciples to go (Matt. 9:35 to 10:1). The sequence of events indicates that concern over the harvest, prayer for the laborers, and willingness to go as a laborer are vitally related in the Christian experience. It is very likely true that no Christian who does not enter first into the work of the Kingdom through the medium of prayer will ever enter effectively in any other way. Witness the people in our churches who have never been inspired to serve God.

However, the pathway of the servant of God is not easy, and discouragement, even after entering, is often a reality. Witness the number of people in our churches who used to be servants but are no longer so. Witness also the number of men who once started out to become preachers of the gospel and fell by the way or quit after discouraging experiences. The answer to discouragement in service is the fellowship of prayer. Two incidents in the life of Paul illustrate this fact. The first is his experience at Corinth on the second missionary journey. Hounded from city to city by his opponents, he came to Corinth and after a few weeks experienced the same surging power of evil in opposition to his work. Though the record does not say he prayed, there can be little doubt that he did. The result was the assurance of the Lord, "Do not be afraid, but speak and do not be silent; for I am with you, and no man shall attack you to harm you; for I have many people in this city" (Acts 18:9–10). The result was that the revitalized apostle continued to preach with power and success in Corinth for a year and more. But would he have had the courage to continue if he had not had his fellowship with the Lord in the season of prayer? Again, when Paul had been taken prisoner and his enemies sought his death, we sense a moment of despair in the great apostle. And again the Lord appeared to him, no doubt during a period of fellowship and prayer, and encouraged him. He said, "Take courage, for as you have testified about me at Jerusalem, so you must bear witness also at Rome" (Acts 23:11). And once more the apostle took heart; his courage did not leave him during five years as a prisoner of the Lord. He labored perhaps more abundantly from prison than when he was free, but his courage to labor came from the Lord.

The next result that may be expected through the practice of prayer is the guidance of God in our service. Guidance that is sometimes contrary to all human expectations and thus guidance that can come only through the fellowship with God in prayer. The experiences of three New Testament men illustrate this point. The first of these is the experience of Philip, who in the midst of a great revival in Samaria received the guidance of the Holy Spirit which led him to the desert of Gaza and to his testimony to, and the consequent conversion of, the Ethiopian eunuch (Acts 8:26–40). While no specific mention of prayer is made in relation to this experience, there can be little doubt that the practice of prayer on Philip's part was essential to it. Notice that no amount of religious surveys or human reasoning would ever have led Philip to make this journey into the desert. His action would never have happened aside from the leadership of God.

Too often the modern Christian thinks of his service in the same terms as that of the insurance salesman, who must depend on human ingenuity and wisdom to achieve his success. The salesman learns by experience and study that if he makes a certain number of calls on prospects, a certain number of sales will, on the average, come as a result. Thus he goes about his task, depending on the law of averages, hoping that his industry and persistence will pay off in results. Some preachers have been guilty of the same practice. We survey the field, locate the prospects, and visit as many persons as we can, with the hope that the law of averages will again result in success. There is nothing wrong with this procedure except that one important element is left out. Before we visit, we should seek the leadership of God. For success, we should depend, not upon the law of averages, but upon the guidance of the Holy Spirit. If our prayer fellowship with God was as close and constant as it should be, we would never make a false step nor an unnecessary visit. We would be led to that person who at that time was in need of and ready to receive our testimony.

This conclusion is enforced by the experience of Peter and Cornelius (Acts, chs. 10 and 11) which we have noticed already. Here the practice of prayer is explicitly mentioned. Cornelius prayed and received instructions to send for Peter; Peter prayed and received enlightenment and guidance to go. The sermon is preached; the Gentiles are saved. Now the church at Jerusalem calls the apostle into question about his fellowship with Gentiles.

His answer, an answer that satisfied the most extreme critics, at least for the time being, was that the whole experience was under the leadership of the Holy Spirit.

In the experience of Paul, the leadership of the Spirit in service in response to prayer is often attested. It was while the elders at Antioch were "worshiping and fasting" (a practice that undoubtedly involves prayer) that the Spirit could say, "Set apart for me Barnabas and Saul for the work to which I have called them." In response to this call of the Spirit, they, "after fasting and praying . . . laid their hands on them and sent them off" (Acts 13:1–3). This whole experience, marking as it does the first foreign mission effort in Christian history, happened as a result of prayer. On his second missionary journey, Paul again found the leadership of the Holy Spirit necessary. After visiting the churches founded on the first journey, Paul and his company were "forbidden by the Holy Spirit to preach the word in Asia." They then attempted to go into Bithynia, "but the Spirit of Jesus did not allow them." Coming to Troas, not knowing where to turn, a vision of the Macedonian man with his cry for help led Paul and his party to set sail for Macedonia, concluding that God had called them "to preach the gospel" to the Macedonians (Acts 16:6–10). Again the practice of prayer is not explicitly mentioned, but who would doubt that these various experiences of the leadership of God did come as a result of the fellowship of prayer? A third incident of a negative kind is recounted by Paul as he sought to convince the Jewish mob of his divine call. No doubt the incident refers to the earliest efforts of Paul to preach, efforts that seemed to him could be best spent in Jerusalem, the scene of his former persecutions of the church. From a human standpoint, this would appear to be the golden opportunity for the former enemy to become the witness to the grace of God. Where else could he serve God so effectively as here? While Paul "was praying in the temple," however, the Lord revealed to him the hopelessness of his purpose and said, "They will not accept your testimony about me" (Acts 22:17–18). In obedience to the leadership of the Lord, Paul left Jerusalem and later launched his Spirit-led career as a missionary to the Gentiles, the results of which are an open book to be read by all.

Guidance is not all that the servant of God needs. If he is to succeed, he must have power. All of us know that this power must come from God; sometimes we forget that it comes as a result of prayer. The conversion of the Philippian jailer emphasizes this relation (Acts 16:25). Paul and Silas prayed and sang praises to God in prison at midnight. The sequence of events that followed is to be explained only by the exercise of divine power. The jailer and his family were led to Christ and became a part of the favorite church of Paul. All because Paul prayed? No. His prayer did not cause the conversion of the jailer; it opened the way for the power of God to operate in Paul and through him for the conversion of the jailer. This is the very point about which we must constantly remind ourselves. Our prayers are not powerful; God is powerful. Our prayers do not prevail; God prevails through us. Our prayers are only the opening of the gates of our hearts to the vital presence of God that makes our service powerful and effective. This is, no doubt, what Jesus meant by his promises of power in service, related as they were to the promise of unlimited resources for service through prayer in his name (cf. John 14:12–14; 15:16). The understanding is what led Paul to write to the Thessalonians and say to them, "Our gospel came to you not only in word, but also in power and in the Holy Spirit and with full conviction" (I Thess. 1:5).

Finally, let us remind ourselves that the essential elements of Christian service cannot be gained in any other way except through the practice of prayer. The Christian who seeks to serve God should do many things. He should seek the highest possible education, both general and religious, not because education guarantees success in service, but because God can work more powerfully through the medium of an educated mind. He should seek to exercise good judgment in making the decisions of life. He should seek to develop a healthy body that can stand the strain of full devotion to a demanding cause. All these are helpful;

none of them will make a Christian a great preacher, missionary, or lay worker. It is only through the fellowship that we have with God through prayer that we receive inspiration, encouragement, guidance, and power in service. Many have forfeited great promise in service because they have not developed the habit of effective prayer. As we serve, therefore, let us pray; and as we pray, let us serve.

Short Studies on Prayer

$\mathbf{C}$an one ever feel that he has done justice to the New Testament teachings on prayer? It is doubtful. When we have considered all the material, we must still feel that we have considered it inadequately. As we seek to make application of the material to the various elements of prayer life, we must confess that we have failed to consider all possible subjects.

This short chapter is an effort to gather up some of the loose ends in our discussion of New Testament material. Some subjects related to the practice of prayer are given scant attention in the New Testament. But some of these have received considerable attention in some Christian circles.

What follows is an effort to consider the relevant teachings of the New Testament in relation to bodily posture in prayer, the wording of our prayers, the place of prayer, the proper attire while praying, and the relation between fasting and prayer. In some instances the results are largely negative; in others they may be helpful.

Bodily Posture in Prayer

Little stress is laid on bodily posture in prayer in the New Testament; there is no prescribed posture to take. This has not always been true in Christian history. Some persons have identified praying with "kneeling"; others, no doubt, have had their own ideas as to the proper physical posture in prayer.

In the New Testament, three positions of prayer or worship are mentioned without any indication that these were required.

Satan promised to give Jesus all the kingdoms of the world if he would fall down and worship him (Matt. 4:9). This reflects the most common Jewish practice in worship. The Greek word that is usually translated "worship" in our English translations literally means to kiss the feet (Greek, *proskuneō*). This would, of course, necessitate the prostration of the worshiper before the person who is worshiped. However, Jesus removed this word from the realm of the purely physical when he told the Samaritan woman that true worship had to be "in spirit and truth" (John 4:24).

Kneeling is also mentioned as a position of prayer in the New Testament. Paul knelt with the elders of Ephesus and prayed with them when he took leave of them (Acts 20:36). Stephen "knelt down and cried with a loud voice" (Acts 7:60) while he was being stoned. Peter knelt and prayed before he raised the disciple named Tabitha (Acts 9:40). Paul's party kneeled on the beach and prayed with the disciples of Tyre as they "bade one another farewell" (Acts 21:5). Paul equated kneeling with praying when he said, "For this reason I bow my knees before the Father, . . . that according to the riches of his glory he may grant . . ." (Eph. 3:14–16). These are the only passages in the New Testament that mention kneeling in relation to prayer. There are also several passages that indicate that men have kneeled before Jesus in requesting his help, but in most of these instances the supplicant looked on Jesus as a prophet rather than as the divine Son of God.

It may be noticed also that "standing" in prayer is mentioned in the New Testament. The disciples were warned against the hypocrisy of Jews who "love to stand and pray in the synagogues and at the street corners" (Matt. 6:5). In the parable against self-righteousness, both the Pharisee and publican (i.e., tax collector) were pictured as standing while they prayed (Luke 18:11, 13). It is improbable that the connection of standing in prayer with warnings against false prayer were meant to condemn the bodily posture. In the case of the publican, his prayer was heard and answered.

If one had to choose, on the basis of the New Testament, the most Christian bodily posture, I suppose he would choose kneeling. Kneeling is most frequently mentioned in relation to prayer; in some of the passages, it is mentioned as if it were the natural and normal position. However, we find that Jesus prayed, at least on occasion, without kneeling. Kneeling is not mentioned with reference to his prayer, and it seems unlikely that he knelt during his prayer on the way to Lazarus' grave or as he prayed in the Temple when the Greeks sought him.

To say the least, there is no positive command concerning the necessity of kneeling when we pray. When this is compared with the emphasis on the necessity of spiritual attitudes, we would have to conclude that kneeling was never thought to be an essential requirement of Christian prayer. It would seem that each man is free to assume the bodily posture that is most helpful to him in his prayer; the essential thing is the spirit of prayer. To some, kneeling might be an aid to true prayer; to others, it might be a hindrance. Many have found prostration of the whole body beneficial when they are most earnest in prayer. Others have prayed best when they stood, sat, or walked around. The only occasion when bodily posture becomes a consideration is when it reveals a proud spirit. One who refused to kneel because he did not want to manifest openly a spirit of humility before God would find it impossible to pray.

Wording of Prayers

The wording of prayers is given scant attention in the New Testament. The only passage that could possibly be called a set formula of prayer is the model prayer. We have already noticed that this was not used liturgically during the New Testament period. When we study the prayers of Jesus and of Paul, we find a wide variety of expressions that would seem to indicate that there was no set formula for prayer.

The only exception to this rule would be the address of prayer. Invariably in the New Testament, when the address is given, God is addressed as "Father." Perhaps this is not so much a matter of form as it is a matter of awareness of the nature of prayer. Prayer is the intimate communion of the child of God with his Father. What more natural than that God should be addressed as Father?

A student of mine once came to me, quite upset, because he found it difficult to think of God as Father. Since the New Testament so often used the term, he felt that he was unchristian in not using it. The word "Father" did not carry pleasant connotations to him. I assured him that I felt that our attitude was a matter of the spirit, not of words. "Father" is, after all, a figure of speech; it points to a truth about the relation of God with his disciples. The primary factor in that relation is its presence, not its expression with a particular word.

Some might ask whether it is at all Christian to use formal prayers in praying. The answer would have to come from the experience of men rather than from the New Testament. The only thing indicated in the New Testament is that formal prayers are not necessary. If one feels that he can pray best if he follows the words of the prayer book, if he really prays when he follows them, I think God would hear his prayer just as surely as he would hear the sincere prayer of the man who prays freely.

The only danger in this practice is the danger of identifying prayer with the repetition of words. If this is the result of using formal prayers, they should be abandoned. One can pray without words, at least with "sighs too deep for words" (Rom. 8:26). On the other hand, an attempt to avoid repetition may become a hindrance to prayer. How could one who gives thanks at meals find new words on each occasion? Striving for variety would be as stultifying to true prayer as slavish devotion would be to formal prayers.

Place of Prayer

I remember spending the night with a farmer once who had a place of prayer. It was a fallen tree trunk just off the footpath that led to the pigpen. Each morning and each evening as he went to feed his pigs, he passed by his place of prayer, was reminded of his need for prayer, and stopped for a while to pray. It was a privilege to share with him a season of prayer in a place that was sanctified by repeated seasons of prayer.

Many persons have found great value in having a specified place of prayer in their homes, in their offices, or on their farms. However, the evidence of the New Testament does not indicate that prayer is peculiarly attached to any place. Jesus made a practice of withdrawing from the multitudes for seasons of prayer. "He withdrew to the wilderness and prayed." (Luke 5:16.) But he also prayed in the midst of crowds (cf. John 11:38–45). When Jesus cleansed the Temple, he said, "It is written, 'My house shall be called a house of prayer'; but you make it a den of robbers" (Matt. 21:13). It is probable that the early Christians continued to visit the Temple at the hours of prayer. "Now Peter and John were going up to the temple at the hour of prayer, the ninth hour." (Acts 3:1.)

Perhaps a word would be in order about the injunction of Jesus to "go into your room and shut the door and pray to your Father who is in secret" (Matt. 6:6). As we have noticed, this constituted a piece of practical advice to guard against display of piety in prayer. We could hardly think of it as specifying a place of prayer as particularly hallowed.

In this matter, it would seem that each Christian is free to pray in any place. He may pray in the wilderness, withdrawn from the multitudes; he may pray in the midst of pressing throngs. He may pray in his home, in the fields, or in the building of his church. Since "the Most High does not dwell in houses made with hands" (Acts 7:48), true communion with him may be found at any place as well as at any time.

Clothes and Prayer

How should a person dress when he prays? This is a question that would seldom if ever be asked. The only reason for asking it now is that it is spoken of in a New Testament passage. "Any man who prays or prophesies with his head covered dishonors his head, but any woman who prays or prophesies with her head unveiled dishonors her head—it is the same as if her head were shaven." (I Cor. 11:4–5.) "Judge for yourselves; is it proper for a woman to pray to God with her head uncovered?" (V. 13.)

This is a strange passage, but if we are to consider the New Testament material on prayer, we must see what it means. The injunction for men to pray unveiled and for women to pray veiled was peculiarly Christian in the first century. Romans worshiped with heads covered; Jewish men veiled their faces in prayer.

We can understand this passage only in the light of the larger context, which speaks of a series of subordinations in the Christian economy. "I want you to understand that the head of every man is Christ, the head of a woman is her husband, and the head of Christ is God." (V. 3.) Notice that this speaks of subordination in function, not of *inferiority*. There is no evidence that Paul thought of Christ as inferior to God the Father, nor that he thought of women as inferior to men. But in the economy of the Christian system, in function, there is subordination. From the beginning the thought that man is to be the head of the house and woman is to be the helpmate has been a part of the Jewish-Christian tradition.

What Paul seems to have been condemning was the effort of women in Corinth to throw off this God-ordained subordination, especially in their religious life. For a woman to have "prayed" with her head uncovered would have been for her to have flaunted the provisions of God for woman's life on earth. Why? The answer lies in the social custom of that day. Among the Greeks only the *hetairai* (the unmarried mistresses of men) went about unveiled. Slave women had their heads shaved; perhaps the shaven head was also the punishment for an adulteress. Thus, for a Christian woman to appear in church with unveiled head would have been tantamount to classing herself with either the immoral or enslaved.

"The woman that unveils her face in public worship shames herself, inasmuch as she declines, to her shame, to wear the badge of her subjection in the Church order to man."[84] "The man," on the other hand, "shames himself by wearing a symbol of subjection to the woman, whereas Christ has given the man supremacy over the woman in the Church order, and that supremacy is expressed by the symbol of an unveiled face."[85] Paul's thought seems to revolve around his conception of the veil as a symbol of divinely ordained status. The important thing is not the symbol but the spirit. To refuse to take the place in the Christian order that God has ordained would be rebellion. This would make prayer ineffective, for it could not be the prayer of faith.

Society changes and symbols change with it. In our world of today, there is left scarcely a single outward indication of any difference between men and women. Few men wear dresses, but some wear skirts. Few women wear trousers all the time, but most do some of the time. It would be difficult to find any regulation that would openly symbolize the subjection of woman unto man. It would probably still hold true that a man who did not seek to fulfill his function in the world would find it difficult to pray effectively. The same would be true of a Christian woman. However, it would seem that this, now more than ever, must be a matter of the spirit rather than a matter of dress. If this is true, no particular dress can be said to be essential to effective prayer.

Fasting and Prayer

To the Jews, fasting was a deed of piety. The Pharisee could boast, "I fast twice a week" (Luke 18:12). Included among the religious practices that Jesus mentioned in his warning against ostentatious display is fasting. His advice on fasting was very similar to his teaching on secret prayer. "And when you fast, do not look dismal, like the hypocrites, for they disfigure their faces that their fasting may be seen by men. Truly, I say to you, they have their reward. But when you fast, anoint your head and wash your face, that your fasting may not be seen by men but by your Father who is in secret; and your Father who sees in secret will reward you." (Matt. 6:16–18.)

The Jewish habit of fasting was no doubt continued by those
who became Christian. This was only natural, and we find
instructions concerning fasting in the Didache, which differ
from Jewish practice only in the fact that the fast days were
Wednesday and Friday rather than Monday and Thursday.[86]
However, we find only one passage in the New Testament where
fasting is mentioned as a Christian practice. "While they were
worshiping the Lord and fasting, the Holy Spirit said, 'Set apart
for me Barnabas and Saul for the work to which I have called
them.' Then after fasting and praying they laid their hands on
them and sent them off." (Acts 13:2–3.) There are textual variations in two other passages that mention fasting in relation to
prayer (cf. Mark 9:29 and I Cor. 7:5), but the best textual
evidence shows that fasting was not in the original manuscripts.
The Greek word for "fasting" (*nēsteia*) is a part of the genuine
text in two other passages, but the word simply means to be
without food. The context of the two passages in which Paul
speaks of his sufferings for Christ would indicate that the RSV
translation of "hunger" (II Cor. 6:5) and "often without food"
(II Cor. 11:27) is correct. Paul would hardly mention religious
fasting as one of the things he had suffered for Christ.

What shall we say regarding the relation of fasting and
effective prayer? It seems that the custom was only incidental
to prayer and was not vital. When Jesus was reproached because
his disciples did not fast as the Pharisees and the disciples of John
did, he seems to have condemned fasting as a religious practice
(Mark 2:18–22; cf. Matt. 9:14–17; Luke 5:33–39). He replied
that his disciples could not fast while he was with them but that
they would fast on the day he was taken from them. He continued, "No one sews a piece of unshrunk cloth on an old
garment; if he does, the patch tears away from it, the new from
the old, and a worse tear is made" (Mark 2:21). His thought
seems to be that Christianity is not to be a "patched up" version
of Judaism; it is to be a new religion, a religion of the spirit
rather than of form.

There seems to be little reason for the remark: "There are

indications that New Testament Christians were specially sensitive to the Spirit's communications during fasting."[87] I would tend to agree with Rackham: "Fasting, then, was not a specially Christian practice. It was really part of the asceticism which was so highly esteemed and inculcated in all the oriental religions: we might almost call it a practice of natural religion in the east. But herein lay its danger. It might (and did) very easily lead to doctrinal error, viz., the belief that matter itself was evil, and also to spiritual pride, together with false ideas about merit and good works. Consequently there is little emphasis laid on fasting in the New Testament."[88]

Fasting as an attendant circumstance of prayer might, in some cases, be helpful. There is no reason to condemn those who think that it is. On the other hand, it would seem to me that fasting would be helpful in prayer only to the extent that one becomes so concerned about some matter that he forgets the normal demands of bodily appetite. Certainly, there is no evidence that fasting is essential to effective prayer.

Addenda: Materials for Study

The following Scripture passages are relevant to the study of prayer in the New Testament.

Matthew	13:18	19:46
5:44	13:33	20:47
6:5–15	14:22–23	21:36
7:7–11	14:32–42	22:17–19
7:21–22	15:34	22:31–32
9:38		22:39–46
11:25–26	*Luke*	23:34
14:19	1:10	23:46
15:8	1:13	24:30–31
18:19–20	1:46–55	24:49
19:13	1:64	
21:13	1:68–79	*John*
21:21–22	2:26–32	4:23–24
24:20	2:36–38	6:11
26:26–27	3:21	9:31
26:36–46	5:16	11:41–42
26:53	5:33	12:27–30
27:46	6:12	14:12–14
	6:28	15:7
Mark	6:46	15:16
1:35	9:16	16:23–27
6:41	9:18	17:1–26
7:6–7	9:28–29	
8:6–7	10:2	*Acts*
10:13–16	10:21	1:14
11:17	11:1–13	1:24
11:23–24	17:18	2:42
12:40	18:1–14	3:1

3:8
4:8–12
4:24–31
6:4
6:6
7:59–60
8:15
8:22–24
9:5–11
9:40
10:4
10:9–16
10:30
11:4–11
11:18
12:5–12
13:2–3
14:23
15:28
15:40
16:6–9
16:13
16:16
16:25
18:9–10
19:6
20:32
20:36
21:14
22:7–11
22:17–21
23:11
26:13–15
27:21–25
28:15

Romans

1:7–9
1:21
8:15
8:26–27
9:1–4
10:1–2

10:9–13
12:12
14:6
15:5–6
15:13
15:30–33
16:25–27

I Corinthians

1:3–7
1:14
2:13
7:5
11:4–5
11:24
14:14–17
14:18
16:23

II Corinthians

1:2
1:3–4
1:11
2:14
4:15
8:16
9:12
9:14
12:6–10
13:7
13:14

Galatians

1:3–5
2:2
4:6
6:18

Ephesians

1:2–3
1:16–17
3:14–19

5:17–20
6:18–20
6:23–24

Philippians

1:2–5
1:9
1:19
2:11
2:13
2:27
3:15
4:6–7
4:11
4:20–23

Colossians

1:2–3
1:9
4:2–3
4:12

I Thessalonians

1:2–3
3:9–13
5:17–18
5:28

II Thessalonians

1:2–4
1:11–12
2:13
2:16–17
3:1–2
3:5
3:16
3:18

I Timothy

1:2
1:12–13
1:17

Notes

1. Norman B. Johnson, *Prayer in the Apocrypha and Pseudepi-qrapha* (Society of Biblical Literature and Exegesis, 1948), p. 3.

2. Emil Brunner, *Revelation and Reason*, tr. by Olive Wyon (The Westminster Press, 1946), p. 408.

3. *Ibid.*, p. 400.

4. *Ibid.*, p. 409.

5. Fred L. Fisher, *The Purpose of God and the Christian Life* (The Westminster Press, 1962), pp. 16–17.

6. O. Hallesby, *Prayer*, tr. by Clarence J. Carlsen (Augsburg Publishing House, 1945), p. 20.

7. W. T. Conner, *Faith of the New Testament* (Broadman Press, 1940), p. 50.

8. John A. Broadus, *Matthew, The American Commentary*, Vol. I (American Baptist Publication Society, 1886), p. 232.

9. B. F. Westcott, *The Gospel According to St. John* (Wm. B. Eerdmans Publishing Company, 1950), p. 173.

10. J. H. Bernard, *Gospel According to St. John*, Vol. II (T. & T. Clark, Edinburgh, 1928).

11. George A. Buttrick, "The Gospel According to St. Matthew," *The Interpreter's Bible*, Vol. 7 (Abingdon Press, 1951), p. 309.

12. Archibald M. Hunter, *A Pattern for Life* (The Westminster Press, 1953), p. 66.

13. Ernst Lohmeyer, *Das Vater-Unser* (Vandenhoeck & Ruprecht, Göttingen, 1960), pp. 52–55.

14. John Wick Bowman and Roland W. Tapp, *The Gospel from the Mount* (The Westminster Press, 1957), p. 122.

15. Sherman E. Johnson, "The Gospel According to St. Matthew," *The Interpreter's Bible*, Vol. 7, p. 310.

16. Brunner, *op cit.,* p. 89.

17. Floyd V. Filson, *A Commentary on the Gospel According to St. Matthew* (Harper & Brothers, 1960), p. 95.

18. Hunter, *op. cit.,* p. 69.

19. Bowman and Tapp, *op. cit.,* p. 125.

20. Hunter, *op. cit.,* p. 70.

21. *Ibid.*

22. Johnson, *op. cit.,* pp. 312, 313.

23. *Op. cit.,* p. 126.

24. Hunter, *op. cit.,* p. 71.

25. *Ibid.*

26. Bowman and Tapp, *op. cit.,* p. 126.

27. Karl Barth, *Prayer,* tr. Sara F. Terrien (The Westminster Press, 1952), p. 59.

28. Bowman and Tapp, *op. cit.,* p. 127.

29. Hunter, *op. cit.,* p. 72.

30. Buttrick, *op. cit.,* p. 314.

31. Leslie D. Weatherhead, *A Private House of Prayer* (Hodder and Stoughton, Ltd., London, 1958), pp. 3–19.

32. Georgia Harkness, *Prayer and the Common Life* (Abingdon Press, 1958), pp. 43–85.

33. Edwyn Bevan, "Petition: Some Theoretical Difficulties," *Concerning Prayer* (Macmillan & Co., Ltd., London, ca. 1916), p. 194.

34. John R. Rice, *Prayer: Asking and Receiving* (Sword of the Lord Publishers, 1942), p. 54.

35. *Ibid.,* p. 50.

36. Rufus Jones, "Prayer and the Mystic Vision," *Concerning Prayer,* p. 118.

37. F. J. Huegel, *Prayer's Deeper Secrets* (Zondervan Publishing House, 1959), p. 37.

38. O. Hallesby, *op. cit.,* pp. 29–30.

39. S. D. Gordon, *Quiet Talks on Prayer* (Grosset & Dunlap, Inc., ca. 1941), pp. 10–27.

40. Carl Van Doren, *Benjamin Franklin* (The Viking Press, Inc., 1938), p. 748.

41. Rom. 15:5–6; Eph. 1:15–19; 3:14–19; Phil. 1:9–11; Col. 1:9–14; 2:1–3; I Thess. 3:11–13; II Thess. 1:11–12.

42. Rom. 1:7; 15:13; 15:33; I Cor. 1:3; 16:23; II Cor. 1:2; 13:14; Gal. 1:3; 6:18; Eph. 1:2; 6:23–24; Phil. 1:2; 4:23; Col. 1:2; 4:18; I Thess. 1:1; 5:28; II Thess. 1:2; 2:16–17; 3:16; 3:18; I Tim. 1:2;

Notes

191

6:21; II Tim. 1:2; 1:16; 1:18; 4:22; Titus 1:4; 3:15; Philemon 3; 25; Heb. 13:25; I Peter 1:2; 5:14; II Peter 1:2; II John 3; III John 15; Jude 2.

43. W. E. Oesterley, "The General Epistle of James," *The Expositor's Greek Testament,* ed. by W. Robertson Nicoll, Vol. IV (Wm. B. Eerdmans Publishing Company, n.d.), p. 473.

44. *Ibid.,* p. 474.

45. Paul Carleton, *Rejoicing in Prayer* (The Messenger Press, ca. 1956), p. 15.

46. Conner, *op. cit.,* pp. 150–151.

47. F. F. Bruce, *The Book of Acts* (Wm. B. Eerdmans Publishing Company, 1956), p. 242.

48. Charles Bigg, *A Critical and Exegetical Commentary on the Epistles of St. Peter and St. Jude* (T. & T. Clark, Edinburgh, 1901), p. 155.

49. R. A. Torrey, *How to Pray* (Fleming H. Revell Company, 1900), pp. 48–49.

50. *Ibid.,* pp. 49–50.

51. Frederick C. Grant, "Exegesis of Mark," *The Interpreter's Bible,* Vol. 7, p. 832.

52. R. A. Torrey, *op. cit.,* p. 41.

53. Floyd V. Filson, *Opening the New Testament* (The Westminster Press, 1952), p. 191.

54. Conner, *op. cit.,* p. 472.

55. Ernest DeWitt Burton, *The Epistle to the Galatians* (T. & T. Clark, Edinburgh, 1921), p. 482.

56. Gordon Poteat, "Exposition of James," *The Interpreter's Bible,* Vol. 12, p. 23.

57. Gordon, *op. cit.,* p. 57.

58. C. K. Barrett, *The Epistle to the Romans* (Harper & Brothers, 1957), p. 168.

59. Karl Barth, *A Shorter Commentary on Romans* (John Knox Press, 1959), p. 102.

60. Howard Rhys, *The Epistle to the Romans* (The Macmillan Company, 1961), p. 111.

61. James Denney, "St. Paul's Epistle to the Romans," *The Expositor's Greek Testament,* Vol. II, p. 651.

62. Conner, *op. cit.,* p. 367.

63. James G. S. S. Thomson, *The Praying Christ* (Wm. B. Eerdmans Publishing Company, 1959), p. 15.

64. Alfred Plummer, *Gospel According to St. Luke,* (Charles Scribner's Sons, 1902), p. 298.

65. S. MacLean Gilmour, "Exegesis of Luke," *The Interpreter's Bible,* Vol. 8, p. 202.

66. A. B. Bruce, "The Synoptic Gospels," *The Expositor's Greek Testament,* p. 548.

67. W. R. Bowie, *et al.,* "Exposition of Luke," *The Interpreter's Bible,* Vol. 8, p. 203.

68. H. K. Luce, *The Gospel According to St. Luke* (Cambridge University Press, 1933), p. 212.

69. Archibald M. Hunter, *Interpreting the Parables* (The Westminster Press, 1961), p. 69.

70. A. B. Bruce, *op. cit.,* p. 596.

71. Hunter, *Interpreting the Parables,* pp. 69–70.

72. J. S. Bonnell, *The Practice and Power of Prayer* (The Westminster Press, 1954), p. 91.

73. Thomson, *op. cit.,* p. 14.

74. Bowie, *et al., op. cit.,* p. 307.

75. *Ibid.*

76. Carleton, *op. cit.,* p. 20.

77. George A. Buttrick, "Exposition of Matthew," *The Interpreter's Bible,* Vol. 7, p. 473.

78. Filson, *A Commentary on the Gospel According to St. Matthew,* p. 202.

79. *Ibid.,* p. 201.

80. Broadus, *op. cit.,* p. 389.

81. Charles B. Williams, *The New Testament* (Bruce Humphries, Inc., 1937), p. 51.

82. Broadus, *op. cit.,* 389.

83. W. F. Arndt and F. W. Gingrich, *A Greek-English Lexicon of the New Testament and Other Early Christian Literature* (The University of Chicago Press, 1957), p. 781.

84. T. C. Edwards, *A Commentary on the First Epistle to the Corinthians* (Hodder and Stoughton, Ltd., London, 1903).

85. *Ibid.,* p. 273.

86. R. B. Rackham, *The Acts of the Apostles* (Methuen & Co., Ltd., London, 1901), p. 190.

87. F. F. Bruce, *op. cit.,* p. 261.

88. Rackham, *op. cit.,* p. 190.